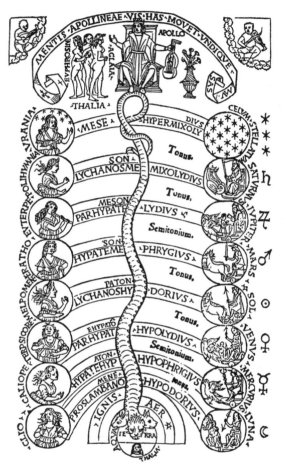

Musica Universalis *from* Gafurius's Practica Musice, *1496. Apollo is shown presiding over the Muses and planetary spheres (left), and tunings and ratios (right). On the left the Three Graces, Euphrosine (mirth), Aglaea (splendor) and Thalia (comedy, also a muse) stand over the other eight muses: Urania (astronomy); Polyhymnia (hymns); Euterpe (music, song & elegiac poetry); Melpomene (tragedy); Terpsichore (dance); Calliope (epic poetry);*

This softcover edition © 2021 by Octavia Wynne
Published by Wooden Books LLC,
San Rafael, California

Hardcover edition first published in the US in 2015
by Bloomsbury Publishing USA, New York

Library of Congress Cataloging-in-Publication Data
Wynne, O.
Poetic Meter and Form

Library of Congress Cataloging-in-Publication
Data has been applied for

ISBN-10: 1-952178-08-8
ISBN-13: 978-1-952178-08-5

Designed and typeset in Glastonbury, UK

Printed in China on 100% FSC
approved sustainable papers by FSC
RR Donnelley Asia Printing Solutions Ltd.

WOODEN
BOOKS

POETIC

METER AND FORM

Octavia Wynne

Thanks to Liz Tetlow, Trent Halliday, John Martineau, Stephen
Parsons, Woody River, Adam Tetlow, & Richard Henry.

Other good books on this subject are: *The Ode Less Travelled*, by
Stephen Fry, 2007, *The Poet's Manual and Rhyming Dictionary*, by
Frances Stillman, 1972, *Poetic Meter and Poetic Form*, by Paul Fussell,
1979, *Poetry, The Basics*, by Jeffrey Wainwright, 2004,
and *Rules for the Dance*, by Mary Oliver, 1998.

Lord, who createdst man in wealth and store,
    Though foolishly he lost the same,
        Decaying more and more,
            Till he became
                Most poore:
                With thee
            O let me rise
        As larks, harmoniously,
    And sing this day thy victories:
Then shall the fall further the flight in me.

My tender age in sorrow did beginne
    And still with sicknesses and shame.
        Thou didst so punish sinne,
            That I became
                Most thinne.
                With thee
            Let me combine,
        And feel thy victorie:
    For, if I imp my wing on thine,
Affliction shall advance the flight in me.

Above: Easter Wings by George Herbert [1593-1633]; an example of a "shaped poem"
(technopaegnion or calligramme), very popular in the 16th and 17th centuries. The earliest
known examples of shaped poems are from Crete, 1700BC, and Egypt, 700BC. The forms
can vary: six surviving ancient Greek examples are shaped as an egg, an axe, wings, an altar
(twice) and a syrinx (shepherd's pipe). Very often the shape of the poem is its subject.

CONTENTS

Above: Après la Marne, Joffre visita le front en auto, *Tommaso Marinetti,*
1915. A visual and sound poem presented like a military map to show the journey
of General Joffre. Visual poems objectify their text and use line length, grouping,
indentation, punctuation, capitalisation, typefaces, and size changes to effect shifts
in tone, topic, and perspective to heighten awareness of the process of reading.

INTRODUCTION

P EOPLE HAVE BEEN WRITING poems for a very long time. The Sanskrit epic *Ramayana* dates to around 300 BC and is still popular throughout India, Cambodia, Indonesia, and Thailand. The Chinese *Shih-ching*, or *Book of Songs*, contains 305 poems dating from the 11th to 7th centuries BC. Poems meaningfully pattern the musical features of language, using rhythm, pitch, and timbre (texture) and often grasp at truths that resist the logical pen of prose. This book looks at the patterns of poetry, its shapes and rhythms, through foot, meter, and form.

The word 'poetry' derives via Latin from the Greek term *poiein* ('to make'). In the Archaic Period [800–480 BC], poetry was largely improvised orally, often accompanied by *music* (derived from the Greek word *mousikê*, 'having to do with the Muses'). In the Classical Period [480–323 BC], poetry began to be performed with the other verbal arts, *rhetoric* (public speaking) and *drama*, and some poems were memorized and written down.

Ancient European poetry was often sung: land songs, Anglo Saxon oar songs, Celtic smith songs, Greek altar songs, medieval court songs, and children's songs. The vast majority of pre-12th century English poetry is lost, but the Anglo-Saxons and Vikings brought with them a canon of verse full of epic myth which rolled and rowed to a four-beat turn with a stress on the first syllables of words, forming an earthy rhythm. Other settlers who followed them sometimes emphasized the ends of words, encouraging rhymes and a lilting upward beat. These two opposing styles combined in the daily rhythms of speech, poetry, and song. Later, the Crusades and the Renaissance brought with them the Greek and Roman classics, encouraging poets of the time to imitate the ancient forms.

1

Patterns in Language

rhythm, meter, rhyme, and form

LISTEN TO PEOPLE SPEAKING in any language and one can immediately detect patterns of various kinds, for language itself is innately suited for song and chant, and its spoken form is an echo of ancient music and poetry.

The most basic pattern of language is its *rhythm*, heard as a beat:

BEAT   1   &   2   &   3   &   4   &

Pít-*ter* **Pát**-*ter* **Pít**-*ter* **Pát**-*ter*

In poetry, rhythm is most clear when spoken aloud, mainly as the effect of *syllables* and *stresses*. The majority of European Romance languages, derived from Latin, are *syllable-timed*, their natural rhythm resting on the number of syllables in words, phrases and sentences.

e.g. French: **Cá-ná-dá** (all syllables stressed equally).

English, on the other hand, is derived from West Germanic languages, and relies heavily on the *stresses* placed on syllables—it is *stress-timed*. It is as though, when walking, the basic rhythmical *left/right* pattern develops a bias towards one or other foot, a little like the way the British often accent the first syllable of a word, while Americans emphasize the second/last:

UK: **Dé**brís US: De**brís**

In *prosody*, these different kinds of rhythmically stressed units are known as *feet*. Add some sway into your walk and a longer foot emerges:

LÉFT, *two, three* | **RÍGHT**, *two, three*

Accented syllables (marked *áéíóúý*) and the feet they define (divided by |) became the foundation of post-13th century English poetry. We will meet the various feet in the pages which follow (*pages 6–13*), and learn how they may be formally combined into a line of two, three, four, five, six, seven, or eight feet, which is then said to have a *poetic meter* (*pages 14–19*).

Poetic lines combine into larger units, *stanzas* (*pages 30–39*), which can be two lines (*couplets*), three (*triplets*), four (*quatrains*), or more, sometimes with occasional lines repeated as *refrains*. A finished poem may contain anywhere between one and over 2,000 stanzas, with some poetic forms dictating exactly how many stanzas are required (*closed* or *fixed forms*), and others allowing the poet more flexibility (*open forms*). The final part of this book examines some of the more popular poetic forms (*pages 40–53*).

There is a second obvious pattern of language: *rhyme*. This might be thought of as a natural phenomenon, since language uses a limited number of sounds to create words, yet two-thirds of the world's languages do not use poetic rhyme. The earliest known use of rhyme dates back to the *Book of Songs* (*see page 1*), and it arrived in Europe from China via Middle Eastern trade routes, through ancient Rome and Persian mystery cults and from Celtic Ireland around the 3rd–4th centuries BC. During the Middle Ages, English poetic rhyme was based on *alliteration*, where words start with the same stressed consonant (*five/feet*); and *assonance*, where words share the same vowel sounds (*black/hat*), but by the 14th century *perfect rhyme* (*bright/night/light*) was found in all European poetry, becoming ubiquitous in English verse around the 16th–17th centuries (*see pages 26–27*).

There are other interesting patterns that words make, and which poets use, and these are explored later in the book (*pages 54–55*). Indeed, the building blocks and tools of poetry are reflections and refinements of natural patterns already present in language. Poetry may require effort and skill to write, but we all experience the simple delight of words which beat and rhyme, and which, at the right time, can find easy passage into hearts and minds.

ACCENTUAL OR SYLLABIC VERSE

all about the rhythm

Meter is counted in different ways. *Accentual* meter is a natural mode of English verse and appears in Irish/Celtic, Old Norse, Anglo-Saxon, and Middle English poetry such as *Beowulf* and *Sir Gawain and the Green Knight*, as well as nursery rhymes, football chants, traditional ballads, and literary imitations (by Coleridge, Hopkins, Yeats, and others). For example:

ACCENTUAL VERSE - EXAMPLE WITH 2 BEATS PER LINE

Báa, baa, bláck sheep,	(4)	Óne for the máster,	(5)
Háve you any wóol?	(5)	And óne for the dáme,	(5)
Yés sir, yés sir,	(4)	And óne for the líttle boy	(7)
Thrée bags fúll;	(3)	Who líves down the láne.	(5)

Note how the number of stresses remains constant despite the changing syllable-count—since accentual verse counts only the stresses in a poetic line there may be any number of weak syllables in any part (*see too page 140*).

Syllabic verse, by contrast, purely counts the number of syllables in a line and is common in syllable-timed languages such as Spanish, French, Italian, the Baltic and Slavic languages, Turkish, Cantonese, and Japanese. For example, Dylan Thomas' 1946 poem *In My Craft or Sullen Art* uses seven syllables in each line but has no regular stress pattern.

SYLLABIC VERSE - EXAMPLE WITH 7 SYLLABLES PER LINE

In my cráft or súllen árt	(7)	I lábour by sínging líght	(7)
Éxercised in the stíll níght	(7)	Nót for ámbition or bréad	(7)
When ónly the móon ráges	(7)	Or the strút and tráde of chárms	(7)
And the lóvers líe abéd	(7)	On the ívory stáges	(7)
With áll their gríefs in their árms,	(7)	Bút for the cómmon wáges	(7)
		Of théir most sécret héart.	(6)

The strictest form of poetic meter is *accentual-syllabic*. Here, both the number of stresses and the number of syllables are fixed. If most lines in a poem have the same number of syllables *and* stresses, or a poem has repeating patterns of them, then it is accentual-syllabic verse, as in this 1963 example from *The Gashlycrumb Tinies*, by Edward Gorey.

ACCENTUAL-SYLLABIC VERSE - DACTYLIC TETRAMETER dúm diddy ●○○ × 4

Á is for| Ámy who| féll down the| stáirs   ●○○ ●○○ ●○○ ●

B́ is for| Básil as|sáulted by| béars   ●○○ ●○○ ●○○ ●

Ć is for| Clára who| wásted á|way   ●○○ ●○○ ●○○ ●

D́ is for| Désmond thrown| óut of a| sléigh   ●○○ ●○○ ●○○ ●

In *quantitative meter*, used in ancient Greek, Roman, and Sanskrit poetry, it is the length of syllables in time that counts. Feet are durational rather than accentual, and each syllable is either long (*longis*) ■ or short (*brevis*) □. Syllables in English are likewise of different lengths, but although these lengths do affect the rhythm of speech, they disappear alongside the strong rhythms created by the patterns of stressed and unstressed syllables. Some Renaissance poets attempted to write English verse in quantitative meter, with limited success. In the example below, from Edmund Spenser's 1579 poem *Iambicum Trimetrum*, notice the rhythms of duration over stresses.

QUANTITATIVE VERSE - QUANTITATIVE IAMBIC TRIMETER di dummm □■ × 3

Un<u>happy</u> verse, the <u>witness</u> of my un<u>happy</u> state,   □■ □■ □■

Make <u>thy self</u> flutt'ring <u>wings</u> of thy <u>fast flying</u>   □■ □■ □■

Thought, and <u>fly forth</u> unto <u>my love</u>, whereso<u>ever she be</u> ... □■ □■ □■

There are a few other examples. However, in this short book, in order to achieve our purpose, we will learn our feet and meters via more easily scannable poems, primarily employing the familiar rhythms of English accentual-syllabic verse.

THE SPONDEE
dum dum

The basic element of meter is a *foot*, which consists of stressed (classically long) and/or unstressed (classically short) beats or syllables. The punchiest of the feet, and the symbol of rhythm itself, is the *spondee*. With two stressed beats, ●●, it KICKS HARD. Rare in poems, you are more likely to hear it in political slogans or football chants, or read it on road signs:

THE SPONDAIC FOOT - dúm dúm (●●)

SLOW DOWN!	●●	GIVE WAY!	●●
TURN RIGHT!	●●	THINK BIKE!	●●

The repetitive stress of the spondee may be heard in stressful situations, e.g. JUMP! JUMP! or compounded as: MAYDAY! MAYDAY! Shakespeare uses it in *Trolius and Cressida*: Crý, crý! Tróy búrns, or élse let Hélen gó.

Spondees are often mixed with less forceful feet to make a point: COME COME *you answer with an idle tongue,* or to create a stop at the end of a line: *True ease in writing comes from art* NOT CHANCE.

Two spondees placed together make a *dispondee*. Examples are the giant's call Fée Fýe Fóe Fúm or the multiple-rhyming Hów Nów BrównCów?

A rare example of a dispondaic poem is E.J. Thribb's 1967 *Bonfire Song*:

DISPONDAIC VERSE - dúm dúm (●●) × 2

Sún shíne| Móon cúrl	●● ●●
Ráin wásh| Eárth whírl	●● ●●
Fíre fórk| Aír fúrl	●● ●●
Sóng bóy| Síng gírl	●● ●●

The spondee is the most insistent syncopation of meter.

THE PYRRHIC
di di

The opposite of the spondee is the *Pyrrhic* foot. Like the hollow victory to which the word now alludes, the pyrrhic consists of two unstressed syllables. Edgar Allan Poe [1809–49] dismissed it entirely as a chimerical foot, an irrational nonentity, for it is almost impossible to construct an entirely Pyrrhic line or poem out of things like:

THE PYRRHIC FOOT - diddy (○○)

is a	○○	*into*	○○
and the	○○	*any*	○○

Instead these little feet work best combined and contrasted with more stressed feet to punctuate the line. Welsh blues poet Dylan Evans combines a Pyhrric foot with a spondee to form a *minor ionic* in *Old Coals*, 1952.

PYRRHIC + SPONDEE = MINOR IONIC - diddy dúm dúm (○○●●)

See a| déad mán	○○ ●●
In a| bláck hóle	○○ ●●
In the| héartbréak	○○ ●●
Of a| lóne sóul	○○ ●●

A spondee *in front* of a Pyrrhic foot creates the rare and exciting *major ionic*:

SPONDEE + PYRRHIC = MAJOR IONIC - dúm dúm diddy (●●○○)

Squéeze tíght,| it's a	●● ○○
Hót níght,| and the	●● ○○

The Pyrrhic foot is suggestive of further hidden rhythms, as well as other syllables which may be so weak as to be silent or missing altogether.

THE TROCHEE
dum di

A poetic unit consisting of a stressed syllable followed by an unstressed one, ●○, is called a *trochee*. In musical terms it is a strong beat followed by a weaker one, a long note preceding a shorter one. Imagine a sergeant major shouting "LEFT *right*, LEFT *right*, LEFT *right*, ...". The emphasis may be slight, but many of us put our best foot first and walk in trochees.

Linguists speculate that there may be a trochaic bias in early childhood, with baby words like *múmmy, dáddy, háppy, cúddle, húngry, bédtime, íPad,* following this pattern. 'Dr.' Theodor Seuss Geisel [1904–91] used it widely:

SIMPLE TROCHAIC VERSE - dúm di (●○)

ONE Fish	●○	BLACK *fish*	●○
TWO Fish	●○	BLUE *fish*	●○
RED Fish	●○	OLD *fish*	●○
BLUE Fish	●○	NEW *fish*	●○

When trochees are compounded they form trochaic verse. Many nursery rhymes use four trochees per line, e.g. *Simple Simon* or:

TROCHAIC TETRAMETER - dúm di (●○) ×4

Péter,| Péter,| púmpkin| éater	●○ ●○ ●○ ●○
Hád a| wífe but| cóuldn't| kéep her	●○ ●○ ●○ ●○

Lines of trochaic meter often lose weak stresses at the ends of lines (*catalectic*), or add extra stresses to the beginnings of lines (*hypercatalectic*):

TROCHAIC TETRAMETER/TRIMETER

Máry| hád a| líttle| lámb	●○ ●○ ●○ ●
Its fléece was| whíte as| snów	○ ●○ ●○ ●

THE IAMB
di dum

The inverse of the trochee is the *iamb*, an unstressed syllable followed by a stressed one, ○●, the most common foot in English verse. Like the trochee, the iamb reflects the natural rise and fall of speech. Words like *behóld, amúse, aríse, eléct, retúrn*, and *insíst* are all iambs. In his poem *Upon His Departure Hence*, Robert Herrick [1591–1679] uses a single iambic foot for each line.

SIMPLE IAMBIC VERSE · di dúm (○●)

Thus Í	○●	As óne	○●	I'm máde	○●
Pass bý	○●	Unknówn	○●	A sháde,	○●
And díe	○●	And góne	○●	And láid	○●

When several iambs are placed one after the other they create an iambic rhythm, *di-dum di-dum di-dum di-dum*. In this satirical example, Samuel Johnson [1709–84] alternates four and three iambs (*a ballad stanza, page 148*):

IAMBIC TETRAMETER/TRIMETER · di dúm (○●) × 3/4

I pút| my hát| upón| my héad,	○● ○● ○● ○●
And wálked| intó| the Stránd,	○● ○● ○●
And thére I mét anóther mán	○● ○● ○● ○●
Whose hát was ín his hánd.	○● ○● ○●

Five iambs form Shakespeare's mighty *iambic pentameter*: If músic bé the foód of lóve play ón. Lines of six and seven are popular too, but why stop there? Here are lines of eight iambs by W. S. Gilbert, from *The Pirates of Penzance*:

IAMBIC OCTAMETER · di dúm (○●) × 8

I ám\| the vé\|ry mó\|del óf\| a mó\|dern Má\|jor-Gé\|nerál,
I've ín\|formá\|tion vég\|etá\|ble, án\|imál,\| and mí\|nerál

THE DACTYL
dum diddy

The *dactyl* is the three-fold equivalent of the trochee, and has a strong beat followed by two weak ones, ●○○. This makes for a waltzing rhythm "ONE two three, ONE two three, ...". Words like *búffalo*, *stráwberry*, *pát-a-cake*, *éverywhere*, *sýnthesis*, and *mérrily* are dactylic. The word *dactyl* comes from the Greek for finger, *daktylos*, since a long bone is followed by two short ones.

Two dactyls form a *double dactyl*, and this forms the basis of a poetic form designed by Anthony Hecht and John Hollander in 1966:

DOUBLE DACTYL - dúm diddy (●○○) ×2

Híggeldy| Píggledy	●○○ ●○○	Féw realístically	●○○ ●○○
Sérgei Rach|máninov	●○○ ●○○	Cán pianístically	●○○ ●○○
Wróte his con|cértos for	●○○ ●○○	Dígitallístically	●○○ ●○○
Hándspans like| wíngs.	●○○ ●○○	Pláy the damned thíngs.	●○○ ●○○

Four dactyls make *dactylic tetrameter*. In *The Bride of Abydos* Lord Byron [1788–1824] omits many unstressed catalectic syllables at the ends of his lines, adding them as hypercatalectic syllables to the beginning of the next:

DACTYLIC TETRAMETER - dúm diddy (●○○) ×4

Knów ye the| lánd where the| cýpress and| mýrtle	●○○ ●○○ ●○○ ●○
Are émblems of| déeds that are| done in their| clíme -	○ ●○○ ●○○ ●○○ ●
Where the ráge of the| vúlture, the| lóve of the| túrtle	○○ ●○○ ●○○ ●○○ ●○
Now mélt into| sóftness, now| mádden to| críme?	○ ●○○ ●○○ ●○○ ●○○
Knów ye the| lánd of the| cédar and| víne,	●○○ ●○○ ●○○ ●
Where the flówers ever| blóssom, the| béams ever| shíne;	○○ ●○○ ●○○ ●○○ ●○○

Six dactyls form *dactylic hexameter*, one of the primary meters of the Classical world, widely used by Homer and Virgil (*see page 18*).

THE ANAPEST
diddy dum

A grouping of three syllables which saves its kick until the end is called an *anapest*. This waltz goes ○○●, *"one two* THREE, *one two* THREE, *one two* THREE, ...".* Anapestic words like *violín, indiréct, misconcéive, realígn,* and *untowárd* are examples of this foot. Two anapests make *anapestic dimeter* and here is Dr. Seuss again, from his 1954 book *Horton Hears a Who*:

ANAPESTIC DIMETER - diddy dúm (○○●) × 2

On the fíf|teenth of Máy	○○● ○○●	In the héat of the dáy	○○● ○○●
In the Jún|gle of Nóol	○○● ○○●	In the cóol of the póol	○○● ○○●

Four anapests form *anapestic tetrameter*, a fine example of which is Lord Byron's *Destruction of Sennacherib*, first published in 1815.

ANAPESTIC TETRAMETER - diddy dúm (○○●) × 4

The Assý\|rian came dówn\| like the wólf\| on the fóld,   ○○● ○○● ○○● ○○●
And his có\|horts were gléam\|ing in púr\|ple and góld;
  And the shéen of their spéars was like stárs on the séa,
  When the blúe wave rolls níghtly on déep Galilée.

A variation appears in the well-known *The Night Before Christmas*, by Clement Clarke Moore [1779–1863]. Note the omission of the first syllables of lines 3 and 4, which produces *acephalous*, or *headless*, lines.

ANAPESTIC TETRAMETER - diddy dúm (○○●) × 4

'Twas the níght\| before Chríst\|mas, when áll\| through the hóuse ○○● ○○● ○○● ○○●
Not a créa\|ture was stír\|ring, not é\|ven a móuse. ○○● ○○● ○○● ○○●
  The stó\|ckings were húng\| by the chím\|ney with cáre, ○○● ○○● ○○● ○○●
  In hópes\| that St Ních\|olas sóon\| would be thére. ○○● ○○● ○○● ○○●

THE AMPHIBRACH
di dum di

The third place where emphasis can fall in a three-syllable unit is in the center, ○●○, to form an *amphibrach*, "one **Two** three, one **Two** three, one **Two** three, ...", as in *imágine, eléctron, impróper, forebéarance, petúnia,* and *corréctly.* Amphibrachs (along with anapests) also form the basis of limericks:

CATALECTIC AMPHIBRACHIC DI/TRIMETER - di dúm di (○●○) × 2/3

There wás an| old mán from| Perú   ○●○ ○●○ ○●

Who dréamed he| was éating| his shóe.   ○●○ ○●○ ○●

  He wóke in| the níght   ○●○ ○●

  With a térri|ble fríght   ○ ○●○ ○●

And fóund that| his dréam had| come trúe!   ○●○ ○●○ ○●

Four amphibrachs gallop along, as here in Dr. Seuss' *If I Ran the Circus*:

AMPHIBRACHIC TETRAMETER - di dúm di (○●○) × 4

And NÓW comes| an áct of| Enórmous| Enórmance!   ○●○ ○●○ ○●○ ○●○

No fórmer perfórmer's perfórmed this perfórmance!

Amphibrachs are a common meter in Russian poetry, where the final syllable is often omitted, as here in Thomas Hardy's *The Ruined Maid*:

CATALECTIC AMPHIBRACHIC TETRAMETER - di dúm di (○●○) × 4

"O 'Mélia|, my déar, this| does évery|thing crówn!   ○●○ ○●○ ○●○ ○●

Who cóuld have| suppósed I| should méet you| in Tówn?

The inversion of the amphibrach is the rare *amphimacer*, ●○●, *dúm-di-dúm*:

AMPHIMACER - dúm di dúm (●○●), from *The Oak*, by Lord Tennyson [1809-92]

Líve thy lífe / Yóung and óld / Líke yon oák / Bríght in Spríng / Líving góld.

	FOOT	LENGTH	KEY	RHYTHM	EXAMPLE
MONO	brach	1	●	strong	*bíg, stár, béat, hóle*
	macer	1	○	weak	*a, the, in, to, by*
BINARY	iamb	2	○●	rising	*alíve, becóme, contról, a bírd, to séek*
	trochee	2	●○	falling	*mústard, pívot, wéaving, fínd it*
	spondee	2	●●	emphatic	*ráinbów, cúckóo, lóve sóng*
	pyrrhic	2	○○	quiet	*any, into, of a, in the*
TERNARY	anapest	3	○○●	rising	*disagrée, incorréct, violín*
	dactyl	3	●○○	falling	*émphasis, flíckering, móckingbird*
	amphibrach	3	○●○	galloping	*eléctron, enchántment, insístence*
	amphimacer	3	●○●	galloping	*místletóe, lá-di-dáh, mén-at-árms*
	bacchius	3	○●●	rising	*abúndánce, my héart áches*
	antibacchius	3	●●○	falling	*óutsíder, flátfóoted*
	molossus	3	●●●	emphatic	*bómbárdmént*
	tribrach	3	○○○	quiet	*anyway, in and out, into it*
QUATERNARY	tetrabrach	4	○○○○	quiet	*innit yeah sis, insy-winsy*
	primus paeon	4	●○○○	galloping	*dífficulties, génuinely, sécularist*
	secundus paeon	4	○●○○	galloping	*abnórmally, comédian, discóvery*
	tertius paeon	4	○○●○	emphatic	*acquisítion, deconstrúction, incohérent*
	quartus paeon	4	○○○●	emphatic	*misunderstánd, undersubscríbed*
	major ionic	4	●●○○	falling	*péjórative, pré-éminent, próféssional*
	minor ionic	4	○○●●	rising	*with the lóve sóng, anacrúsis*
	ditrochee	4	●○●○	falling	*círculátion, ídiótic, váriátion*
	diiamb	4	○●○●	rising	*levíathán, buffóonerý, assíduóus*
	choriamb	4	●○○●	galloping	*múrmuring sílk, óde to the wést,*
	antispast	4	○●●○	galloping	*besíde bóttom, abóve cótton*
	first epitrite	4	○●●●	emphatic	*tomáto sóup! behóld Kíng Bíll!*
	second epitrite	4	●○●●	rising	*chóco yúm yúm, háppy bírthdáy!*
	third epitrite	4	●●○●	galloping	*fóotbáll inspíres, píck úp that gún*
	fourth epitrite	4	●●●○	falling	*chíldhóod swéetheart, báthróbe fálling*
	dispondee	4	●●●●	emphatic	*wígwám súnshíne, básebáll tóothbrúsh*

METER
dimeter and trimeter

Poetic feet combine to produce poetic *meter,* and each meter has its own distinctive quality, melody, and musical meaning. Likewise, a subject, mood, or feeling may suggest an appropriate meter. In general, meters are formed from a single repeated foot, although some meters are combinations of different feet (*e.g. the Sapphic, see page 48*).

Meters are named after the Greek number and type of foot of which they are comprised; thus with one foot per line a poem is described as being in *monometer* (*see examples on pages 8–9*) and with two feet per line it is an example of *dimeter,* and so on. Such simple meters are rare outside children's verse. However, lines of three feet, *trimeter,* are more common.

Here is some iambic trimeter from William Blake's 1777 *I Love the Jocund Dance* (note the hypercatalectic syllable at the start of the fourth line).

IAMBIC TRIMETER - di dúm (o●) × 3

I lóve| the jóc|und dánce,	o● o● o●
The sóft|ly bréa|thing sóng,	o● o● o●
Where ínn|ocent éyes| do glánce,	o● o● o●
And where lísps| the mái|den's tóngue.	oo● o● o●

The waltzing quality of trimeter is doubly apparent in this poem by William Cowper, published in 1782:

ANAPESTIC TRIMETER - di di dúm (oo●) × 3

I am óut| of humán|ity's réach,	oo● oo● oo●
I must fín|ish my jóur|ney alóne,	oo● oo● oo●
Never héar| the sweet mú|sic of spéech;	oo● oo● oo●
I stárt| at the sóund| of my ówn.	oo● oo● oo●

Meter	No.	FOOT		SYLL.	EXAMPLE
Dimeter	2	Trochaic	●○ × 2	4	Úp the válleys / Dówn the cányons
	2	Iambic	○● × 2	4	And só to dréam / How still the dáy
	2	Anapaestic	○○● × 2	6	From the céntre all sóund / and all silence is fóund
	2	Dactylic	●○○ × 2	6	Cánnon to right of them / Cánnon to léft of them
Trimeter	3	Trochaic	●○ × 3	6	Glíding clóse to héaven / sóaring óver Dévon
	3	Iambic	○● × 3	6	The ónly néws I knów / is búlletíns all dáy
	3	Anapaestic	○○● × 3	9	And I láugh to see thém whirl and flée
	3	Dactylic	●○○ × 3	9	Túrning and gálloping wéarily
Tetrameter	4	Trochaic	●○ × 4	8	Bý the shóres of Gítchee Gúmee
	4	Iambic	○● × 4	8	And báts went róund in frágrant skíes
	4	Anapaestic	○○● × 4	12	The Assýrian came dówn Like the wólf on the fóld
	4	Dactylic	●○○ × 4	12	Grínd away, móisten and másh up thy páste I say
Pentameter	5	Trochaic	●○ × 5	10	Sítting sínging quíetly bý the ríver
	5	Iambic	○● × 5	10	And súmmer's léase hath áll too shórt a dáte
	5	Anapaestic	○○● × 5	15	Like the ówl in the níght who was thínking some míce might be níce
	5	Dactylic	●○○ × 5	15	Chórus oh sing with the sún as she ríses and shínes on us
Hexameter	6	Trochaic	●○ × 6	12	Hóly, hóly, hóly, áll the sáints adóre thee
	6	Iambic	○● × 6	12	Did nów but fréshly spríng, and silken blóssoms béare
	6	Anapaestic	○○● × 6	18	As a slóop with a swéep of immáculate wíngs on her délicate spíne
	6	Dactylic	●○○ × 6	18	Fáint was the áir with the ódorous bréath of magnólia blóssoming
Heptameter	7	Trochaic	●○ × 7	14	Cúrsèd bé the sickly fórms that érr from hónest náture
	7	Iambic	○● × 7	14	Oh sóme are fónd of Spánish wíne and sóme are fónd of Frénch
	7	Anapaestic	○○● × 7	21	For the móon never béams without bringing me dréams of the béautiful Ánnabel Lée
	7	Dactylic	●○○ × 7	21	Dówn in the válley of Ávon so péaceful, so périlous, wáited young Willoughby
Octameter	8	Trochaic	●○ × 8	16	Thén, methóught, the áir grew dénser, pérfumed fróm an únseen cénser
	8	Iambic	○● × 8	16	My sélfish héart its véil now rípped, yet rhýthm héals what bróken stríps
	8	Anapaestic	○○● × 8	24	As a pínnacle cárven and gílded of mén; for the dáte of its dóom is no móre than an hóur's
	8	Dactylic	●○○ × 8	24	Hére is a wónderful cúmbersome spéctacle strúggling to próve it is crédibly póssible

TETRAMETER
four foot

Lines of four feet are known as *tetrameter* (Greek *tetra* is 'four'). These often alternate with lines of trimeter, the paired lines adding to form *ballad heptameter*, as in this example from Macaulay's *Lays of Ancient Rome*:

IAMBIC TETRAMETER / TRIMETER - di dúm (o●) × 4/3

Then óut| spake bráve| Horá|tiús,	o● o● o● o●
The Cáp|tain óf| the Gáte:	o● o● o●
"To évery mán upón this éarth	o● o● o● o●
Death cómeth sóon or láte."	o● o● o●

We have already seen examples of trochaic, anapestic, dactylic, anapestic, and amphibrachic species of tetrameter (*pages 8–12*), but here is another interesting variety from *Lucy In the Sky With Diamonds*, by Lennon & McCartney, whose elongated 'trees' and 'skies' almost put it in the category of accentual verse (*see page 4*).

DACTYLIC TETRAMETER - dúm diddy (●oo) × 4

Pícture your|sélf in a| bóat on a| ríver	●oo ●oo ●oo ●o
With tángerine| trée-ees and| mármalade| skí-ies	o ●oo ●oo ●oo ●oo
Sómebody cálls you, you ánswer quite slówly	●oo ●oo ●oo ●o
A gírl with kaléidoscope| éyes	o ●oo ●oo ●

Longer feet (*see page 13*) can create great rhythms. Here is contemporary poet Julia Donaldson, with the first two lines from *Tyrannosaurus Drip*:

TERTIUS PAEONIC TETRAMETER - diddy dúm di (oo●o) × 4

In a swámp be\|side a ríver\| where the lánd was\| thick with vég
Lived a hérd of\| duck-billed díno\|saurs who róamed the\| waters édge.

PENTAMETER
five feet

Five feet make a line of *pentameter*, and five iambs form *iambic pentameter*, the beating heart of most traditional English metrical poetry since the 14th century. This is a *measured meter*, the 'heroic' line of English verse from Chaucer and Shakespeare to the present, used to translate the epic dactylic hexameter of Homer's *Iliad* and *Odyssey* and Virgil's *Aeniad* into English. Take these two lines from Shakespeare's *Sonnet 18*:

IAMBIC PENTAMETER - di dúm (o●) × 5

Rough wínds| do sháke| the dárl|ing búds| of Máy,
And súmmer's leáse hath áll too shórt a dáte.

Examples of *trochaic pentameter* are very rare, so instead let's turn to another popular meter from classical Greek and Latin poetry, the *dactylic pentameter*. This line was made of two equal parts, each consisting of two dactyls and a stressed half-foot, the number of feet summing to five in total, and with the first half-foot always ending a word, to produce a *caesura* (*see page 20*). Classical quantitative meters do not translate well into English (*see page 5*), but here is an attempt at the form in English accentual-syllabic style:

DACTYLIC PENTAMETER - dúm diddy (●oo) × 5

"Whát is the| póint of you| Sír?" ¶ said the| Kíng, almost| víolently.
"Whý are there stárs in the ský?" ¶ then he láughed and stood sílently.

In the *elegiac couplet* (*see page 49*) a line of dactylic pentameter follows a line of dactylic hexameter. Ovid's *Amores*, a collection of erotic poems about love, begin with Cupid stealing a metrical foot from Ovid's epic hexameter, then turning it into pentameter to create the compound form.

HEXAMETER
the six footer

Six iambic feet produce a hypnotic line, *iambic hexameter*, also known as an alexandrine, which tends to divide itself in half. Here is a sample from Michael Drayton's 15,000-line epic *Poly-Olbion*, published in 1612:

IAMBIC HEXAMETER - di dúm (o●) × 6

Consí|der, quóth| this Nýmph,| the tímes| be cúr|ious nów,
And nó|thing óf| that kínd| will án|y wáy| allów.
The móre they hér persuáde, the móre she dóth persíst;
Let thém say whát they wíll, she wíll do whát she líst.

The classical quantitative meter (*see page 5*) is the six-foot *dactylic hexameter*. In Homer's epic poems, any of the first four dactyls can be substituted (*see page 22*) with spondees (*see page 6*) while the sixth foot is a spondee or trochee. The Greek form was approximated in English by Henry W. Longfellow in his 1847 poem *Evangeline*. Notice his substitutions and final spondees.

DACTYLIC HEXAMETER - dúm diddy (●oo) × 6

Thís is the| fórest pri|méval. The| múrmuring| pínes and the| hémlócks,
Béarded with| móss, and in| gárments| gréen, indis|tínct in the| twílight,
Stánd like| Drúids of| óld, with| vóices| sád and pro|phétic,
Stánd like| hárpers| hóar, with| béards that| rést on their| bósoms.

Anapestic hexameter has a lovely galloping quality. W. B. Yeats used it for Book III of his epic *Wanderings of Oisin*, first published in 1889:

ANAPESTIC HEXAMETER - diddy dúm (oo●) × 6

And thére| at the fóot| of the móun|tain, two cár|ried a sáck| full of sánd ...
Leaning dówn| from the gém|-studded sád|dle, I flúng| it five yárds| with my hánd

HEPTAMETER & OCTAMETER
seven and eight feet

Seven feet form lines of exciting *heptameter*. These can often be divided into one part trimeter and one part tetrameter. Emily Dickinson [1830–86] often used iambic heptameter within ballad stanzas:

IAMBIC HEPTAMETER - di dúm (o●) ×7

Becáuse| I cóuld| not stóp| for Déath,| He kínd|ly stópped| for mé;
The cárr|iage héld| but júst| oursélves| and Ímm|ortá|litý.

Sevens and threes often go well together and here are two anapestic lines from Lewis Carroll's *The Hunting of the Snark*, published in 1876.

ANAPESTIC HEPTAMETER - diddy dúm (oo●) ×7

"He remárked| to me thén,"| said that míld|est of mén,|"If your Snárk| be a Snárk,| that is ríght:
Fetch it hóme| by all méans|—you may sérve| it with gréens,| and it's hán|dy for strí|king a líght.

Eight feet form an *octameter*. In Edgar Allan Poe's 1845 poem *The Raven*, the first line can be cut in half to form a double tetrameter whilst the second line is true octameter (with a few dactylic substitutions):

TROCHAIC OCTAMETER - dúm di (●o) × 8

Ónce, up|ón a| mídnight| dréary,| while I| póndered| wéak and| wéary
Óver| mány a| quáint and| cúrious| vólume| óf for|gótten| lore

Combining eight anapests produces a very long line, as in this example from Algernon Charles Swinburne's 1887 poem *March, an Ode*:

ANAPESTIC OCTAMETER - diddy dúm (oo●) × 8

Ere fróst-flower and snów-blossom fáded and féll and the spléndour of wínter had pássed out of síght,
The wáys of the wóodlands were fáirer and stránger than dréams that fulfíl us in sléep with delíght;

CAESURA
take a breath

A break or audible pause in the flow of a line is called a '*caesura*', ¶, from the Latin *caedere*, 'to cut'. Caesurae can vary or support poetic rhythm, and create expressive contrasts, both metrical and rhetorical. Often marked with punctuation, they are like breath pauses between musical phrases. A caesura near the beginning of a line is termed *initial*, near the middle is *medial*, and near the end is *terminal*. In the extracts below from *Paradise Lost*, John Milton [1608–74] makes flexible use of initial and terminal caesurae:

INITIAL AND TERMINAL CAESURA - in iambic pentameter (o●) di dúm × 5

Séasons| retúrn,| but nót| to mé| retúrns
Dáy, ¶ or| the swéet| appróach| of Év'n| or Mórn.

Gó in| thy ná|tive ínn|océnce, ¶ relíe
On whát| thou hást| of vér|tue, ¶ súmm|on áll,

Medial caesurae are usually less idiosyncratic. They neatly aid stylistic/contextual counterpoint and, in the absence of strict meter, can help define rhythm (they are an ever-present feature in *Anglo-Saxon* verse, *see p. 51*). Here is Thomas Nashe's c. 1587 poem *Spring, the Sweet Spring*:

MEDIAL CAESURA (RHYTHMICAL) - in catalectic dactylic tetrameter (●oo) dúm diddy × 4

Spríng, the sweet| spríng, ¶ is the| yéar's pleasant| kíng,
Thén blooms each| thíng, ¶ then maids| dánce in a| ríng,

In Alexander Pope's 1731 *Moral essay*, caesura augments antithesis:

MEDIAL CAESURA (RHETORICAL) - in accentual
Cháste to her Húsband, ¶ fránk to all besíde,
A téeming místress, ¶ but a bárren Bríde.

STOP OR ENJAMB
the end of the line

In a single line of verse, *end-stopping*, ⊙, marks the end of a complete phrase. This usually coincides with suitable punctuation, though sometimes the sense of the words alone dictates the pause. End stopping is a principle element of rhythm, sense, and form in most English poetry. Here are four end-stopped lines from Elizabeth Browning's *A Musical Instrument*, 1854:

END STOPPING - in dactylic trimeter (●○○) dúm diddy × 4

Whát was he| dóing, the| gréat god Pán, ⊙
  Dówn in the| réeds by the| ríver? ⊙
Spréading rúin and scáttering bán, ⊙
  Spláshing and páddling with hóofs of a góat, ⊙

When a line runs onto the next and the reader feels little compulsion to pause, it is said to be *enjambed*, ✓, (from the French *enjamber* 'to stride'). Here are two enjambed lines from Maya Angelou's [1928–2014] poem *Rise*:

ENJAMBMENT - in anapestic/quartus-paeonic dimeter (○○○●) diddy dúm × 2

Does it cóme| as a surprise ✓
  That I dánce like I've got díamonds ✓
At the méeting of my thíghs?

Here are both devices, in a verse from Andrew Marvell's *The Mower to the Glo-Worms*, published in 1781:

END STOPPING & ENJAMBMENT - in iambic tetrameter (○●) di dúm × 4

Ye cóun|try cóm|ets, thát| porténd ✓
  No wár| nor prín|ce's fún|erál, ⊙
Shíning untó no hígher énd ✓
  Than tó preságe the gráss's fáll; ⊙

SUBSTITUTION
changing feet

A poetic line which ends with an unstressed syllable is said to have a *feminine ending*, whereas one with a final stressed syllable is *masculine*. To aid *lineation* (the flow of lines) an iambic or anapestic line will occasionally end with an extra unstressed syllable. For example, this extract from Shakespeare's *Hamlet*, published in 1603, although written in iambic pentameter (5 iambic feet, 10 syllables per line), contains *hypermetrical* lines of 11 syllables:

ADDING FEMININE ENDINGS - to iambic pentameter (o●) di dúm × 5

Thus cón|science dóes| makeców|ards óf| us áll; ⊙	(10) *m*
And thús| the ná|tive húe| of rés|olútion ⌄	(11) +*f*
Is síck| lied ó'er| with the| pále cást| of thóught, ⊙	(10) *m*
And én|terprí|ses óf| gréat píth| and móment ⊙	(11) +*f*

Note that the longer lines still consist of five feet, and that the addition of the unstressed syllable to the final foot changes it from an iamb into an amphibrach (*see page 12*). Deeper scansion of the above also reveals that this is not the only change in foot type. For example, a pyrrhic foot (*see page 7*) 'with the' appears in the third line, and a spondaic 'great pith' in the fourth.

This *substitution* of one foot for another is a commonly-used technique in metrical verse. A poet exchanges the expected foot for a different one, even of a different length. The swap is often found at the beginning of lines but can occur anywhere, any number of times. Here is Hamlet again:

SUBSTITUTION - in iambic pentameter (o●) di dúm × 5

To bé,| or nót| to bé;| thát is| the quéstion:— ⊙	(11) *4th foot trochee*, +*f*
Whéther| 'tis nó|bler ín| the mínd| to súffer ⌄	(11) *1st foot trochee*, +*f*
The slíngs| and á|rrows óf| outrá|geous fórtune; ⊙	(11) *no subs*, +*f*

Ór to| take árms| agáinst| a séa| of tróubles, ⊙   (11) *1st foot trochee, +f*
And bý| oppósing,| énd them?|—To díe|, to sléep ⌣   (11) *2nd amphibr., 3rd troch., m*
Nó móre;| and, bý| a sléep,| to sáy| we énd ⌣   (10) *1st foot spondee, m*
The héart|-áche, and| the thóu|sand nát|ural shócks ⌣   (10) *2nd foot trochee, m*
That flésh| is héir| to,—'Tís| a cón|summátion   (10) *no subs, +f*

Sometimes it can make sense metrically and dialectically to substitute the first foot of a line. For example, in the above extract the opening trochaic 'Whether' (*facing page*) naturally follows a feminine ending. Substitution is also often used expressively, to signal a rhetorical shift, as in Hamlet's forceful opening spondee 'No more' (*above*).

Below, Emily Dickinson emphasizes the opening word of her 1891 poem *Hope is the thing with feathers* with a trochee:

INITIAL SUBSTITUTION - in iambic trimeter (○●) di dúm × 3

Hópe is| the thíng| with féathers ⌣   (7) *1st foot trochee, +f*
that pérch|es ín| the sóul ⊙   (6) *no subs, m*

And here, Robert Frost [1874–1963] uses some *trisyllabic substitution* (the substitution of a binary for a ternary foot, e.g. an anapest for an iamb) in his 1916 poem *The Road Not Taken*:

TRISYLLABIC SUBSTITUTION - in iambic tetrameter (○●) di dúm × 4

Two róads| divérged| in a yé|llow wóod, ⊙   (9) *3rd foot anapest, m*
And sór|ry I cóuld| not tráv|el bóth ⌣   (9) *2nd foot anapest, m*
And bé| one trável|er, lóng| I stóod ⌣   (9) *2nd foot amphibrach, m*
And lóoked| down óne| as fár| as I cóuld ⊙   (9) *4th foot anapest, m*

Thus, with an ear for how language is spoken, metrical variation is part of poetic meter. It is used expressively, expanding and reinforcing meaning, and helping to naturalize a poem's rhythm. Ballads and nursery rhymes tend to vary less, as their meters are reinforced by musical rhythm (*overleaf*).

MORE COMPLEX RHYTHMS
and mixed meters

We have already seen how stresses and syllables create poetic rhythm. Yet something else underpins this art; something deeply connected to the musical origins of poetry. It is background beat, and we all meet it as children in the song and chant of nursery rhymes.

To take an example, *Hickory Dickory Dock* is a five-line accentual poem (*see page 4*), with varying syllable counts, and three stresses for lines 1, 2, and 5, and two for lines 3 and 4. However, when presented in semi-musical notation (*below*) we quickly discover the hidden 3:4 rhythm which is heard when the rhyme is actually spoken:

RHYTHMIC ACCENTUAL

1	2	3	1	2	3	1	2	3	1	2	3	
Híck--or---y			Díck--or---y			Dóck					The	(7)
móuse	ran	úp	the	clóck							The	(6)
clóck		struck óne;		The móuse			ran	dówn				(8)
Híck--or---y			Díck--or---y			Dóck						(7)

Notice how the stressed syllables fall on primary beats while the off-beats host unstressed syllables. In many places neither is marked. *Humpty Dumpty* has a similar rhythm, with lines 3 and 4 marking every beat:

1	2	3	1	2	3	1	2	3	1	2	3	
Húmp----ty			Dúmp----ty			sát	on	a	wáll			(8)
Húmp----ty			Dúmp----ty			hád	a	great	fáll			(8)
Áll the king's hórs---es			and áll			the king's mén						(10)
Cóuldn't put Húmp-ty			to---gé---ther			a---gáin						(10)

Many accentual poems can be analyzed in this way. In *The Owl and the Pussycat*, by Edward Lear [1812–88], the waltzing rhythm is established from the start. It's almost impossible to read the first line without introducing pauses between 'went' and 'to sea', or between 'pea' and 'green boat':

	1	2	3	1	2	3	1	2	3	1	2	3	
The	Ówl	and	the	Pús---sy---cat		wént		to	séa	in	a		(10)
	Béau--ti---ful	péa		green	bóat				They				(8)
	tóok		some	hó---ney	and	plén---ty	of	món---ey	wrapped				(11)
	úp	in	a	fíve		pound	nóte						(7)

Another way that poets vary the contours of metrical schemes is to mix meters. William Wordsworth, in his 1804 ode on *Intimations of Immortality*, appears to change his meter on almost every line, whilst always retaining the lilting iambic foot as his base unit (*this poem also appears on page 49*):

MIXED METER   IAMBIC

There wás| a tíme| when méa|dow, gróve,| and stréam,	pentameter	(10)
The éarth,| and év|ery cóm|mon síght,	tetrameter	(8)
To mé| did séem	dimeter	(4)
Appá|relled ín| celés|tial líght,	tetrameter	(8)
The gló|ry ánd| the frésh|ness óf| a dréam.	pentameter	(10)
It ís| not nów| as ít| hath béen| of yóre; —	pentameter	(10)
Turn whére|soe'er| I máy,	trimeter	(6)
By níght| or dáy,	dimeter	(4)
The thíngs| which Í| have séen| I nów| can sée| no móre.	hexameter	(12)

In the poem below, e e cummings [1894–1962] takes the opposite approach, varying his feet, whilst always ensuring there are four per line:

whát if a| múch of a| whích of a| wínd,	dactylic tetrameter	(10)
gíves the| trúth to| súmmer's| líe;	trochic tetrameter	(7)
blóodies with| dízzying| léaves the| sún	dactylic tetrameter	(10)
and yánks| immór|tal stárs| awrý?	iambic tetrameter	(8)

RHYME
and its schemes

The terms 'rhyme' and 'rhythm' both come from the Greek word *rhythmos* meaning 'flow', 'regular motion', or 'symmetry'. Rhymes bind poetic elements together, creating patterns across space and through time, and implying and intensifying connections. Here's a rhythmic tail rhyme from the end of *The Cat in the Hat* by Dr. Seuss:

END OR TAIL RHYME - anapestic tetrameter (○○●) diddy dúm × 4

Then our mó|ther came ín| and she sáid| to us twó	○○● ○○● ○○● ○○● [a]
'Did you háve| any fún|? Tell me, whát| did you dó?'	○○● ○○● ○○● ○○● [A]
And Sá|lly and Í| did not knów| what to sáy.	○● ○○● ○○● ○○● [b]
Should we téll her the thíngs that went ón there that dáy?	○○● ○○● ○○● ○○● [b]
Should we téll her abóut it? Now whát should we dó?	○○● ○○● ○○● ○○● [A]
Well, whát would you dó if your móther asked yóu?	○● ○○● ○○● ○○● [a]

To notate *rhyming schemes*, each new rhyme is given a letter when it first appears in a poem. In the example above, *a* rhymes with *a*, and *b* with *b*, while repeated end-words are notated with capitalized letters, *aAbbAa*.

Gerald Manly Hopkins' *The Windhover*, 1877, uses alliteration, consonance, end-rhymes, internal rhymes, imperfect rhymes and many other devices:

INTERNAL RHYMES - sprung rhythm, loose pentameter

I *caúght*\| this *mórn*\|*ing mórn*\|*ing's mín*\|*ion, kíng-*
   dom of *dáylight's dáuphin, dápple-dawn-drawn* Fálcon, in his *ríding*
  Of the *rólling* lével underneáth him *stéady aír*, and *stríding*
Hígh there, how he rúng upón the *réin* of a *wímpling wíng*
In his *écstasy!* then *óff, óff fórth* on *swíng*,
   As a *skáte's héel swéeps* smóoth on a *bów-bénd*: the *húrl* and *glíding*
  Re*búffed* the *bíg wínd*. My heárt in *híding*
Stírred for a *bírd*, — the *achíeve* of; the *mástery* of the *thíng*!

RHYME	DEFINITION	EXAMPLE
END OR TAIL RHYME, RIME COUÉE	A rhyme in the final syllable(s) of two or more lines.	The cow is of the bovine ilk One end is moo; the other milk. O. Nash
INTERNAL RHYME	Two or more rhyming words occur within the same line or across the center and / or end words of adjacent lines.	Whát would the wórld be; ónce beréft Of wét and of wíldness? Lét them be léft G.M. Hopkins
CROSS RHYME	The end-word of one line matches a word in the middle of the following line or vice versa.	And he shall go where time lies still and frozen beneath eternal snow.
PERFECT, FULL OR TRUE RHYME	The sound of two words are identical except at the beginning.	light / night; fire / briar; names / flames; fish / dish; kind / mind; hole / mole
MASCULINE	Stress is on the final syllable of each word.	sublime / design; reveal / conceal;
FEMININE	Stress is on the second from last syllable of each word.	thúnder / asúnder; súltry / poúltry; tówers / flówers
DACTYLIC:	Stress is on the third from last syllable of each word.	cacóphony / heteróphony
PARTIAL OR HALF RHYME	Words which almost rhyme. Any species other than perfect rhyme: barn / large, craft / laugh, love / blush, etc	Courage was mine; and I had mystery; Wisdom was mine; and I had mastery: W. Owen
IMPERFECT RHYME	The otherwise perfect rhyming of stressed-unstressed syllables.	Lasting / sting; imagine / grin; summer / her; mountain / win; crystal / fall; narrative / live
ASSONANT RHYME OR ASSONANCE	Vowel sounds are identical but consonants differ.	love / move / prove; oar / oak; blows / notes; round / drown
CONSONANT RHYME	Outer consonants are the same but vowels differ.	night / nought; fell / fall / fool / foul / fail / feel; years / yours
ALLITERATION	Words in close succession have the same first letter or sound.	concordant / consonants / consistently / convolve and aurally / accord
EYE RHYME	A typographic rhyme between words with similar spellings but different sounds.	look / moon / o; thought / though; love / prove; brow / crow; hubris / debris; live / live
RICH RHYME	Rhyme between identical sounding words with different meanings.	their / there; bear / bare; foul / fowl; where / wear; eye / I; see / sea
DIMINISHING RHYME	A perfect chiming of two succesive words where the second is nested in the first.	report / port; emotion / motion; avail / veil; impale / pale; start / art; cracking / king

THE STANZA
unit of poetic form

Syllables combine to form words, words form lines, and lines form *stanzas* (*It.* for 'room'). Stanzas are the building blocks of poetic form, building space, shape, sense, and story in a poem, and aiding the reader's eye. Here are the first two stanzas of Emily Dickinson's *In the Garden* [1891]:

STANZA I
A bírd| came dówn| the wálk:
    He díd| not knów| I sáw;
He bít| an án|gle-wórm| in hálves
    And áte| the féll|ow, ráw.

STANZA II
And thén| he dránk| a déw
    From á| convé|nient gráss,
And thén| hopped síde|wise tó| the wáll
    To lét| a bée|tle páss.

The Greek word for stanza is *strophe*, which means 'turn' (literally, a complete turn in a dance). A poem formed from several stanzas is said to be *strophic*, which in music means several repeated verses (AAA) of the same melody, but with changing lyrics. Successive stanzas can function as introduction, development, and conclusion, much like a story's beginning, middle, and end, or a logical argument (*syllogism*: if P and Q then R).

When starting a poem, a poet faces a choice—whether to use a *fixed form*, a traditional pattern, or a *nonce form*, a unique pattern devised by the poet.

FIXED FORM - e.g. a VILLANELLE, see p.42, first two stanzas, by Dylan Thomas, 1952

Do nót| go gén|tle ín|to thát| good níght,	[A¹]
Old áge| should búrn| and ráve| at clóse| of dáy;	[b]
Ráge, ráge| agáinst| the dý|ing óf| the líght.	[A²]
Though wise men at their end know dark is right,	[a]
Because their words had forked no lightning they	[b]
Do not go gentle into that good night.	[A¹]

28

BLANK VERSE
fewer rules

Poetry which is not *stanzaic*, or broken into stanzas, is *stichic* (pr. *stik-ik*), and poems of unrhymed stichic lines written in regular meter are known as *blank verse*. It has been estimated that three quarters of all English poetry is in blank verse, mostly iambic pentameter. The lack of rhyme is well-suited to argument, emotion, and rhythmic speech. It was first adapted to English from the 11-syllable Italian form *verse sciolti da rima* ('verse free from rhyme') by Henry Howard, Earl of Surrey for his 1540s translations of *The Aeneid*. Christopher Marlowe [1564–93] then used it in *Tamburlaine the Great* before, coupled with rhyme and song, it became the great workhorse of Shakespeare's [1564–1616] plays and Milton's [1608–74] *Paradise Lost*.

Here is an example from Coleridge's *Frost at Midnight*, written in 1768:

BLANK VERSE - using iambic pentameter (o●) di dúm × 5

My bábe| so béau|tifúl!| it thrílls| my héart
With tén|der glád|ness, thús| to lóok| at thée,
And thínk| that thóu| shalt léarn| far ó|ther lóre,
And ín| far ó|ther scénes!| For Í| was réared
In the great city, pent 'mid cloisters dim,
And saw nought lovely but the sky and stars.
But thou, my babe! Shalt wander like a breeze
By lakes and sandy shores, beneath the crags
Of ancient mountain, and beneath the clouds,

Since the late 19th century, some poets have discarded meter as well as rhyme, resulting in *free verse*. This builds form and narrative using rhetoric, repetition, assonance, strophic and stichic line grouping, visual shape, trope, metaphor, and simile, but is not the subject of this book.

Couplets and Triplets
and the terza rima

The *couplet* is the simplest of all stanzas. Formed from any two lines rhyming *aa*, couplets take many forms. In an *equal couplet*, both lines have the same number of syllables and beats. Seventeenth-century poets, Shakespeare among them, often used sequences of couplets in iambic pentameter (known as *heroic couplets*) to give the feel of the classical heroic epics:

HEROIC COUPLET - iambic pentameter (o●) di dúm × 5

The Tíme| is óut| of jóint,| O cúr|sed spíte   [a]
That é|ver Í| was bórn| to sét| it ríght.   [a]

This is also an example of a *closed couplet*, one that forms a complete, balanced statement or sentence. The first line rises/calls; the second answers/falls. Closed couplets can become *epigrams*, like Coleridge's eponymous example:

CLOSED COUPLET - example in iambic pentameter (o●) di dúm × 5

What ís| an ép|igrám?| A dwárf|ish whóle,   [a]
Its bó|dy bré|vitý,| and wít| its sóul.   [a]

Unequal couplets have unequal line lengths, like the *poulter's measure*:

UNEQUAL COUPLET - e.g. the POULTER'S MEASURE, iamb. hex./hept. (o●) di dúm × 5/6

A twélv|ish twíst|ing líne,| a póul|ter's méa|sure kéeps,   [a]
With fóur|teen móre| right ún|dernéath| on whích| the óth|er sléeps. [a]

Two couplets enjambed together are *open couplets*, as in this by Keats [1818]:

OPEN COUPLETS - example in iambic pentameter (o●) di dúm × 5

A thíng| of béau|ty ís| a jóy| for éver: +f [a]
Its lóve|linéss| incréa|ses; ít| will néver ⌄   +f [a]

30

Pass ín|to nóth|ingnéss;| but stíll| will kéep   [b]
A bów|er quíet| for ús,| ¶ ánd| a sléep   [b]

A *triplet* is a three-line stanza of any length, rhyming *aaa*. It is often used for dramatic emphasis and variation in couplet-heavy verse. In *The Eagle*, Tennyson's powerful triplets draw out the bird:

TRIPLETS - example in iambic tetrameter (○●) di dúm × 4

TRIPLET

He clásps| the crág| with cróok|ed hánds: [a]
Clóse to| the sún| in lóne|ly lánds,   [a]
Rínged with| the áz|ure wórld,| it stánds.   [a]

The wrínkled séa benéath him cráwls;   [b]
He wátches fróm his móuntain wálls,   [b]
And líke a thúnderbólt he fálls.   [b]

A *tercet* is any three-line unit of poetry, but when rhymed *aba* it is known as a *terza rima* (Italian for 'third rhyme'). Strung together in *chain rhymes*, *aba bab cdc ded efe* etc., stanzas of terza rima form the backbone of Dante's *Divine Comedy* and Chaucer's *Complaint to His Lady*. Four chained tercets with a concluding couplet, *aba bab cdc ded ee*, form a *terza rima sonnet*.

TERZA RIMA - in iamb. pent. from *Second Satire* by Thomas Wyatt [1503-42]

TERCET

Ye dó| misséek| with móre| travái| and cáre.   [a]
    Make pláin| thy héart,| that ít| be nót| knottéd   [b]
With hópe| or dréad;| and sée| thy wíll| be báre   [a]

    From áll afféts whom více hath éver spótted.   +f [b]
Thysélf contént with thát is thée assígned,   [c]
    And úse it wéll that ís to thée allótted.   +f [b]

Then seek no more out of thyself to find   [c]
    The thing that thou hast sought so long before,   [d]
For thou shalt feel it sitting in thy mind;   [c]

THE BALLAD
the great quatrain

Any four-line stanza is called a *quatrain*. Hugely popular, many English poems are in quatrains: nursery rhymes, songs, and hymns. For example, Robert Burn's 18th century version of *John Barleycorn* begins like this:

THE BALLAD STANZA · iambic tetrameter/trimeter

There wás| three kíngs| intó| the eást,	○● ○● ○● ○●	[a]
Three kíngs| both gréat| and hígh,	○● ○● ○●	[b]
And théy have swórn a sólemn óath	○● ○● ○● ○●	[c]
John Bárleycórn should díe.	○● ○● ○●	[b]

This quatrain is a *ballad stanza* (from the French *ballare*, 'to dance'), which alternates between lines of iambic tetrameter and trimeter. Its lines can rhyme *abcb defe* (as above), use a tighter cross-rhyme *abab cdcd*, or fall into couplets *aabb ccdd*. There are also versions which vary in line-length and meter (a 6-line version, rhyming *abcbdb*, is common). The earliest written English example of the form, *Judas*, dates to at least the 13th century:

Júdas,\| thou móst\| to Júr\|selém,   Thrítti pláten of sélver thóu
  oure mét\|e fór\| to búgge;   bére up óthi rúgge.

Traditional ballads use everyday speech and song to tell stories of love, rural life, work, local events, the supernatural, and the like. The ancient Scottish Border ballad of *Tam Lin* shows the form:

O Í\| forbíd\| you, mái\|dens á',   There's náne that gáes by Cárterháugh
  That wéar\| gowd ón\| your háir,   But théy leave hím a wád,
  To cóme\| or gáe\| by Cárt\|erháugh, Either their ríngs, or gréen mantlés,
  For yóung\| Tam Lín\| is thére.   Or élse their máidenhéad.

The ballad form was used for catchy hymns in the 15th and 16th centuries, when it became known as *common* or *short measure*. Then, between the 17th and 19th centuries, *Broadside ballads* flourished throughout Europe. Printed cheaply, posted on pub walls, and sold by peddlars, they often later became popular songs, passed on orally. Broadside ballads are journalistic, full of sensational news, disaster, love scandals, murder, and suicide. An example is the *Ballad of George Barnwell*, published in the 1650s. Here is an extract:

Most súdd|enlý| withín| a wóod
  he strúck| his Ún|cle dówn
And béat| his bráins| out óf| his héad,
  so sóre| he cráckt| his crówn:

And fóurscore póund in réady cóyn,
  out óf his Púrse he tóok,
And cómming únto Lóndon stráit,
  the Cóuntry qúite forsóok.

Literary ballads developed throughout the 18th century. Oscar Wilde [1854–1900] adapted the form for *The Ballad of Reading Gaol* with two extra lines broadly rhyming *ababcb*, but perhaps the most famous example comes from Coleridge [1722–1834], in *The Rime of the Ancient Mariner*:

All ín| a hót| and cóp|per ský,
  The blóod|y Sún,| at nóon,
Right úp| abóve| the mást| did stánd,
  No bígg|er thán| the Móon.

Dáy after dáy, dáy after dáy,
  We stúck, nor bréath nor mótion;
As ídle ás a páinted shíp
  Upón a páinted ócean.

Much rap, performance poetry, and modern pop uses the ballad form. Here is a ballad variation from Benjamin Zephaniah's *Talking Turkeys*, 1994. Instead of 4-3-4-3 iambic feet, it uses 3-3-4-3 anapestic, much like a limerick:

BALLAD VARIATION - anapestic trimeter/tetrameter (○○●) diddy dúm × 3/4

So, be níce| to yu túr|key dis chrístmas
  Invíte| dem indóors| fe sum gréens
Lét| dem eat cáke| an lét| dem partáke
  In a pláte| of orgán|ic grown béans,

Be níce to yu túrkey dis chrístmas
  An spáre dem de cút of de knífe,
Join Túrkeys Uníted an déy'll be delíghted
  An yú will mek néw friends 'FOR LÍFE'.

FOUR QUATRAINS
four-line stanzas

Long measure is a common quatrain which contains four lines of four iambs with the same *abcb* rhyme scheme as the ballad. T. S. Eliot [1888–1965] used it for *Sweeney Among the Nightingales*, where the form's sincerity and natural openness help reinforce the poems irony:

LONG MEASURE - 4 lines of iambic tetrameter (o●) di dúm × 4

Ápe|neck Swée|ney spréads| his knées	[a]
Létting| his árms |hang dówn| to láugh,	[b]
Déath and| the Rá|ven dríft| abóve	[c]
Swélling| to mác|uláte| giráffe.	[b]
The circles óf the stórmy móon	[d]
Slide wéstward towárd the Ríver Pláte,	[e]
The zébra strípes alóng his jáw	[f]
And Swéeney gúards the hórnèd gáte.	[e]

When long measure has the rhyme scheme *abba*, it is called the *In Memoriam stanza,* after Tennyson's famous lengthy elegy *In Memoriam* [1850], forever associating it with the lyric of loss and lament, as in this extracted quatrain from Section LXXXV:

THE IN MEMORIAM STANZA - 4 lines of iambic tetrameter, rhyming *abba*

This trúth| came bórne| with bíer| and páll,	[a]
I félt| it, whén| I sórr|ow'd móst,	[b]
'Tis better to have loved and lost,	[b]
Than never to have loved at all	[a]

This is also an example of an *envelope stanza,* because the enclosed couplet *bb* is enveloped between another enclosing couplet, *aa.*

The *heroic* or *elegiac quatrain* uses iambic pentameter and has an alternating rhyme scheme *abab*. An example is *Elegy Written in Country Churchyard*, by Thomas Grey [1716–71] (an elegy in name but not in form, *see page 49*):

HEROIC QUATRAIN - 4 lines of iambic pentameter, rhyming *abab*

The cúr|few tólls| the knéll| of pár|ting dáy,	[a]
The lów|ing hérd| wind slów|ly óe'r| the léa,	[b]
The plóughman hómeward plóds his wéary wáy,	[a]
And léaves the wórld to dárkness ánd to mé;	[b]
Now fades the glimmering landscape on the sight,	[c]
And all the air a solemn stillness holds,	[d]
Save where the beetle wheels his droning flight,	[c]
And drowsy tinklings lull the distant folds;	[d]

Notice how the longer lines of the pentameter allow adjectives, fanfare and modifiers of all kinds to come rushing in to fill out the rhythm.

Ruba'i (plural *ruba'iat*) is a traditional Persian quatrain form, which was introduced to England in Edward FitzGerald's 1859 translation of the *Ruba'iat of Omar Khayyam*. Here are two quatrains (from over 1,000), which demonstrate the Ruba'i's rhyming scheme *aaba bbcb ccdc dded etc*:

RUBA'I - 4 lines of iambic pentameter, cross-rhyming with the next 4

Come fíll| the Cúp,| and ín| the Fíre| of Spríng	[a]
The Wín|ter Gár|ment óf| Repén|tance flíng:	[a]
The Bírd| of Tíme| has bút| a lít|tle wáy	[b]
To flý| — and Ló!| the Bírd| is ón| the Wíng.	[a]
And lóok — a thóusand Blóssoms wíth the Dáy	[b]
Woke — ánd a thóusand scátter'd ínto Cláy:	[b]
And thís first Súmmer Mónth that bríngs the Róse	[c]
Shall táke Jamshýd and Káikobád awáy.	[b]

QUINTAINS
limericks and madness

Any poetic form built on five-line stanzas is called a *quintain*. The most widely recognized example in English verse is the *limerick*, which is constructed from three lines of anapestic/amphibrachic trimeter (lines 1, 2, & 5) and two of dimeter (lines 3-4). The rhyme scheme is strictly *aabba*, and the form seems to lends itself particularly well to wit or humour, with extra points awarded for uncanny or ridiculous rhymes, and nonsense or smut.

LIMERICK - Anon, catalectic amphibrachic trimeter/dimeter (o●o) di dúm di × 3/2

There wás a| young lády| named Whíte	[a]
Who trávelled| much fáster| than líght,	[a]
She sét out| one dáy	[b]
In a réla|tive wáy	[b]
And cáme back| the prévi|ous níght	[a]

Five-line stanzas also appear in other *nonsense verse* like 16th- and 17th-century *mad-songs* or *Bedlamite verse*. This form has five lines of variable meter (trochees and anapests) rhyming *abccb*, leaving an unrhymed *a*:

MAD-SONG STANZA - Anon. 16th C.

Fróm the hág and húngry góblin	[a]	
That ínto rágs would rénd ye,	[b]	
All the spírits that stánd	[c]	
By the náked mán,	[c]	
In the bóok of móons defénd ye!	[b]	

QUINTAIN / COUPLET / QUATRAIN

A five-line stanza can be rhymed using the enclosing and enclosed couplets (*as above*), or it can rhyme *ababa*, or *aaaba*, or *abbba*, or it can be simply split into a triplet and a couplet, *aaabb*.

SESTETS
six lines

Stanzas of six lines, *sestets*, can be formed in many ways. Three couplets rhyming *aabbcc* are common, as is the Middle-English *romance stanza*, which rhymes *aabccb*. Scottish poet Robert Burns [1759–96] wrote over fifty poems in sestets; here is the first stanza of his *To a Mountain Daisy*:

THE BURNS STANZA ('STANDARD HABBIE') - iamb. tetr./dimeter (○●) di dúm × 4/2

Wee, mó|dest crím|son-típp|èd flów'r,	[a]
Thou's mét| me ín| an é|vil hóur;	[a]
For Í| maun crúsh| amáng| the stóure	[a]
Thy slén|der stém:	[b]
To spáre| thee nów| is pást| my pów'r,	[a]
Thou bón|ie gém.	[b]

Couplets added to a longer stanza can form an epigram or conclusion, and six lines of iambic pentameter rhyming *ababcc* form the sestet at the end of a *Petrarchan sonnet (page 40)*, a six-line stanza also used by Shakespeare for his 1593 poem *Venus and Adonis*. Sir Walter Raleigh [1552–1618] opted for the same scheme in *The Lie*, but shortened the line to iambic trimeter, while William Wordsworth [1770–1850] used it in tetrameter to describe his famous daffodils in *I Wandered Lonely as a Cloud*:

QUATRAIN WITH END COUPLET - e.g. in iambic tetrameter (○●) di dúm × 4

Contín|uous ás| the stárs| that shíne,	[a]	QUATRAIN
And twín|kle ón| the míl|ky wáy,	[b]	
They strétched in néver-énding líne	[a]	
Alóng| the már|gin óf| a báy:	[b]	
Ten thóu|sand sáw| I át| a glánce,	[c]	COUPLET
Tóssing| their héads| in spríght|ly dánce.	[c]	

SESTET

SEPTETS, OCTAVES, & NINES
for royals and faeries

With seven lines of iambic pentameter rhyming *ababbcc*, the *Rhyme Royal* stanza was introduced into English poetry from late Medieval French court poetry by Geoffrey Chaucer [1343–1400]. He used it for high-minded and comic narratives like the *Parliament of Foules* and *The Canterbury Tales*, while Shakespeare used it for *The Rape of Lucrece*. Here is verse 132 from Book V of Chaucer's *Troilus and Criseyde*:

RHYME ROYAL - 7 lines of iambic pentameter (o●) di dúm × 5

And wíth| that wórd| he gán| to wáx|en réed,	[a]
And ín| his spéche| a lí|tel wíght| he quóok,	[b]
And caste a-syde a litel wight his heed,	[a]
And stinte a whyle; and afterward awook,	[b]
And soberly on hir he threw his look,	[b]
And seyde, 'I am, al be it yow no Ioye,	[c]
As gentil man as any wight in Troye.'	[c]

SEPTET · QUATRAIN · COUPLETS

The scheme hinges on its center (like a musical scale's 4th and 5th), as the *bb* couplet expands the opening quatrain and suggests the *cc* couplet. The fifth line is the pivot—it can expand, amplify, or slow down the broader rhythm of the stanza. This openness makes it well-suited to shifting temporal experiences like dreams, visions, reverie, and trance. Milton added a foot at the end, to give a 12-syllable line (or *alexandrine, see page 134*).

With eight lines, *Ottava Rima* first appeared in Italy in the poetry of Giovani Boccaccio [1313–75], most notably in *The Decameron*. It uses feminine-ended (*see page 22*) lines of iambic pentameter (so *hendecasyllabic*, 11 syllables) and an *ababab cc* rhyme scheme (rhyme royal with an extra fifth line). Simultaneously narrative and meandering, sincere and comic, Lord

Byron [1788–1824] called it 'half-serious rhyme' and used it for his long satirical poem *Don Juan*. Here is a stanza from Canto XVI, in which Don Juan, frightened by a ghost, reflects on his existence:

OTTAVA RIMA - 8 lines of iambic pentameter

Betwéen| two wórlds| life hó|vers líke| a stár   [a]
  'Twixt níght| and mórn,| upón| the horí|zon's vérge   [b]
How little do we know that which we are!   [a]
  How less what we might be! The eternal surge   [b]
Of time and tide rolls on, and bears afar,   [a]
  Our bubbles; as the old burst, new emerge,   [b]
Lash'd from the foam of ages; while the graves   [c]
Of empires heave but like some passing waves.   [c]

OCTAVE / SESTET / COUPLET

The nine-line *Spenserian stanza* was invented by Edmund Spenser [1553–1599] for the *The Fairie Queen*, and was revived in the 19th century by Byron, Keats, Shelley and others. The rhyming scheme is *ababbcbcc*, essentially two chain-rhymed ballad stanzas *abab bcbc* with a concluding *c* to form a couplet. The stanza is formed of eight lines of iambic pentameter and a concluding line of iambic hexameter, a 12-syllable alexandrine. *The Faerie Queen* contains over 2,000 of such stanzas; here is one of them:

SPENSERIAN STANZA - 8 lines of iambic pentameter + 1 line of iambic hexameter

For wéll| I wóte| thou spríngst| from án|cient ráce   [a]
  Of Sáx|on kíngs,| that háve| with mígh|tie hánd   [b]
And many bloody battailes fought in place   [a]
  High reard their royall throne in Britane land,   [b]
  And vanquisht them, unable to withstand: [b]
From thence a Faerie thee unweeting reft,   [c]
  There as thou slepst in tender swadling band,   [b]
And hér| base Él|fin bróod| there fór| thee léft.   [c]
  Such mén| do Cháunge|lings cáll,| so cháng'd| by Fáe|ries théft. [c]

SPENSERIAN / QUATRAIN / QUATRAIN / COUPLET / COUPLET

THE SONNET
fourteen lines of love

The *sonnet* is a 14-line closed poem in iambic pentameter, traditionally on a *lyrical*, or personal, theme, often love. Initially developed in Sicily (*sonetto*, 'a little sound/song'), it was popularized by Francesco Petrarca [1304–74], who divided the stanza 4:3 into an octave (split into two quatrains) followed by a sestet, rhyming *abba abba cdcdcd*, with the sestet occasionally varying as *cddcdc* or *cdecde*. Here is Thomas Wentworth Higginson's [1823–1911] translation of Petrarca's *Gli Occhi Di Ch' Io Parlai*:

PETRARCHAN SONNET - 14 lines of iambic pentameter (o●) di dúm × 5

Those éyes,| 'neath whích| my páss|ionate ráp|ture róse,	[a]
The árms,| hánds, féet,| the béau|ty thát| erewhíle	[b]
Could my own soul from its own self beguile,	[b]
And in a separate world of dreams enclose,	[a]
The hair's bright tresses, full of golden glows,	[a]
And the soft lightning of the angelic smile	[b]
That changed this earth to some celestial isle,	[b]
Are now but dust, poor dust, that nothing knows.	[a]
And yet I live! Myself I grieve and scorn,	[c]
Left dark without the light I loved in vain,	[d]
Adrift in tempest on a bark forlorn;	[c]
Dead is the source of all my amorous strain,	[d]
Dry is the channel of my thoughts outworn,	[c]
And my sad harp can sound but notes of pain.	[d]

OCTAVE: first two quatrains (QUATRAIN, QUATRAIN). SESTET: last six lines. ↳ = volta.

Typically, the first and second quatrains outline and expand upon the subject of the poem (*exposition* and *development*). Then comes the *volta* or 'turn', ↳, often signalled with a preposition '*and*', '*but*', *while*, '*yet*', '*though*', or '*until*', after which the sestet opposes and resolves the subject (*conclusion*).

The *Spenserian sonnet* was developed by Edmund Spenser from the 9-line stanza he used for *The Faerie Queen* (*page 39*). The 14 lines are divided into three chained quatrains and a final couplet, rhyming *abab bcbc cdcd ee*, with the *volta* either after the first octave or before the final couplet.

The *Shakespearean sonnet* became popular around 1600. It is similar to the Spenserian, but easier to rhyme as it separates the three quatrains: *abab cdcd efef gg*. The *volta* is again at the start of the 9th or 13th line, with the final rhyming couplet often acting as an epigrammatic solution to the problem developed over the three quatrains. Here is Shakespeare's *Sonnet 18*:

SHAKESPEAREAN SONNET · 14 lines of iambic pentameter

Shall Í| compáre| thee tó| a súm|mer's dáy?	[a]
Thou árt| more lóve|ly ánd| more tém|peráte.	[b]
Rough winds do shake the darling buds of May,	[a]
And summer's lease hath all too short a date.	[b]
Sometime too hot the eye of heaven shines,	[c]
And often is his gold complexion dimmed;	[d]
And every fair from fair sometime declines,	[c]
By chance, or nature's changing course, untrimmed;	[d]
But thy eternal summer shall not fade,	[e]
Nor lose possession of that fair thou ow'st,	[f]
Nor shall death brag thou wand'rest in his shade,	[e]
When in eternal lines to Time thou grow'st.	[f]
So long as men can breathe, or eyes can see,	[g]
So long lives this, and this gives life to thee.	[g]

QUATRAIN · QUATRAIN · QUATRAIN · COUPLET

Some *sonnet variations* do not follow the rhyming schemes listed above. A famous example is *Ozymandias*, by Percy Shelley [1792–1822], which rhymes *abab acdc edefef*, an interesting fusion of the two classical forms. John Milton's *When I Consider How My Light Is Spent* is another example.

VILLANELLE
nineteen lines

The dreamy rustic *villanelle* (It. *villano* 'peasant' or 'villa') is a closed form of 19 lines of iambic pentameter, with five 3-line stanzas and a final quatrain:

VILLANELLE – 19 lines of iamb. pent: e.g. The Waking, by T. Roethke [1908-63]

1.	I wáke| to sléep,| and táke| my wá|king slów.	A¹
	I féel| my fáte| in whát| I cán|not féar.	[b]
	I léarn| by gó|ing whére| I háve| to gó.	A²
			TERCET
2.	We think by feeling. What is there to know?	[a]
	I hear my being dance from ear to ear.	[b]
	I wake to sleep, and take my waking slow.	A¹
			TERCET
3.	Of those so close beside me, which are you?	[a]
	God bless the Ground! I shall walk softly there,	[b]
	And learn by going where I have to go.	A²
			TERCET
4.	Light takes the Tree; but who can tell us how?	[a]
	The lowly worm climbs up a winding stair;	[b]
	I wake to sleep, and take my waking slow.	A¹
			TERCET
5.	Great Nature has another thing to do	[a]
	To you and me; so take the lively air,	[b]
	And, lovely, learn by going where to go.	A²
			TERCET
6.	This shaking keeps me steady. I should know.	[a]
	What falls away is always. And is near.	[b]
	I wake to sleep, and take my waking slow.	A¹
	I learn by going where I have to go.	A²
			QUATRAIN

A little like a musical round, the 1st and 3rd lines of the first stanza, A¹ and A², are *refrains*, and repeat throughout the poem (*see too page 28*).

Pantoum

strange refrains

The *pantoum* is another circular creature, this time from Malaysia via France. The English adaption has an *open form* composed with a variety of meters in interlocking cross-rhymed quatrains: *abab bcbc cdcd ... jaja*.

The second and fourth lines of each stanza repeat as the first and the third of the next, and the first and third lines of the first stanza become the fourth and second lines of the final stanza. The second half of each quatrain also has a more personal voice than the first half. Here's an extract from *The Blue Fly Sung in the Pane* by Austin Dobson [1840–1921]:

PANTOUM - example in dactylic trimeter (●○○) dúm diddy × 3

1.	Tóiling in| Tówn now is| "hórrid,"	A¹
	(Thére is that| wóman a|gáin!)—	B¹
	Júne in the| zénith is| tórrid,	A²
	Thóught gets| drý in the| bráin.	B²
2.	There is that woman again:	B¹
	"Strawberries! fourpence a pottle!"	C¹
	Thought gets dry in the brain;	B²
	Ink gets dry in the bottle.	C²
3.	"Strawberries! fourpence a pottle!"	C¹
	Oh for the green of a lane!—	D¹
	Ink gets dry in the bottle;	C²
	"Buzz" goes a fly in the pane! ...	D²
10.	To dash one with eau de Cologne,	I¹
	(June in the zenith is torrid;—)	A²
	And why should I stay here alone!	I²
	Toiling in Town now is "horrid."	A¹

BALLADE, TRIOLET, & RONDEAU
French song and dance

The solemn *ballade* is one of the three musical *formes fixes* of medieval French poetry (the other two were the *virelai* and the *rondeau*). The ballade uses 28 lines of consistent meter in three 8-line stanzas rhyming *ababbcbC*, with a closing four line *envoi* rhyming *bcbC*. The last line of the first stanza becomes a refrain, repeated as the last line of all other stanzas, including the *envoi*. Here is the end of Algernon Charles Swinburne's *A Ballad of Dreamland*:

BALLADE - 3 × 8 lines, with a 4-line *envoi*, example in iambic/anapestic tetrameter

3.	The gréen| land's náme| that a chárm| enclóses,	[a]
	It né|ver was wrít| in the tráv|eller's chárt,	[b]
	And swéet| on its trées| as the frúit| that gróws is,	[a]
	It né|ver was sóld| in the mér|chant's márt.	[b]
	The swá|llows of dréams| through its dím| fields dárt,	[b]
	And sléep's| are the túnes| in its trée|-tops héard;	[c]
	No hóund's| note wák|ens the wíld|wood hárt,	[b]
	Ónly| the sóng| of a séc|ret bírd.	C
ENVOI 4.	In the wórld| of dréams| I have chó|sen my párt,	[b]
	To sléep| for a séa|son and héar| no wórd	[c]
	Of trúe| love's trúth| or of líght| love's árt,	[b]
	Ónly| the sóng| of a séc|ret bírd.	C

The jaunty *virelai* is constructed from a 4-line refrain, rhyming AAAB, ABAB, or ABBA, followed by three tercets, rhyming *aab* or *abb*. The refrain repeats and another three tercets and refrain may or may not follow.

The *triolet* is an epigrammatic lyric form, originally sung as two melodies, matching its refrains. With no fixed meter or length, it is usually written in octaves with line 1 repeated as the 4th and 7th, and line 2 as the 8th:

TRIOLET - example in iambic tetrameter by Robert Bridges [1844-1930]

When fírst| we mét,| we díd| not gúess   A

 That Lóve| would próve| so hárd| a máster; +f B

Of more than common friendliness   [a]

When first we met we did not guess   A

Who could foretell the sore distress,   [a]

 This irretrievable disaster,   +f [b]

When first we met? We did not guess   A

 That Love would prove so hard a master. +f B

The triolet is the basis for the *rondeau*, which originated from sung dance-rounds (rondels). The 12- and 15-line variations are the most common. Cut the second line of each stanza from Don Marquis' [1878–1937] 15-line example below to convert it to the 12-line form:

RONDEAU - example in iambic tetrameter (○●) di dúm × 4

Your rón|deau's tále| must stíll| be líght —   [a] R

[No bú|gle-cáll| to lífe's| stern fíght!]   [a]

 Rather| a smi|lling int|erlude   [b]

 Memór|ial tó| some trán|sient móod   [b]

Of íd|le lóve| and gá|la-níght.   [a]

Its manner is the merest sleight   [a]

[O' hand; yet therein dwells its might,]   [a]

 For if the heavier touch intrude   [b]

  Your rondeau's stale.   R

Fragrant and fragile, fleet and bright,   [a]

[And wing'd with whim, it gleams in flight]   [a]

 Like April blossoms wind-pursued   [b]

 Down aisles of tangled underwood; --   [b]

Nor be too serious when you write   [a]

  Your rondeau's tail!   R

SESTINA
lyrical symmetry

The *sestina* is a closed form built on repetition. Mostly unrhymed, it uses any meter for its six 6-line stanzas and final 3-line closing *envoi*. Each stanza juggles the end-words in the next by a pattern: 1→2, 2→4, 3→6, 4→5, 5→3, 6→1. Here is an extract from *Sestina* by Elizabeth Bishop [1911–1979]:

SESTINA - 6 × 6 lines, with a 3-line *envoi*, example in loose iambic tetrameter

1.	Septém|ber ráin| fálls on| the hóuse.	1
	In the fái|ling líght|, the óld| grándmother	2
	síts in| the kít|chen wíth| the chíld	3
	besíde| the Lít|tle Már|vel Stóve,	4
	réading| the jókes| from the ál|manác,	5
	láughing| and tálking| to híde| her téars.	6
2.	She thinks that her equinoctial tears	6
	and the rain that beats on the roof of the house	1
	were both foretold by the almanac,	5
	but only known to a grandmother.	2
	The iron kettle sings on the Stove.	4
	She cuts some bread and says to the child, ...	3
ENVOI 7.	Time to plant tears, says the almanac.	6, 5
	The grandmother sings to the marvelous Stove	2, 4
	and the child draws another inscrutable house.	3, 1

After six stanzas all end-words have rotated through all positions, and then the final *envoi* reuses them in three lines, in the order: 6, 5; 2, 4; 3, 1. The sestina was developed by Arnaut Daniel [fl.1180–1200], one of the *Troubadours*, a southern European group of lyrical poets who sung their poetry over simple monophonic music, shaping the poetic experience.

CANZONE
heads and tails

Canzone, 'song', is the term for various Italian forms derived from medieval Provençal poetry. Stanzas contain between 8 and 20 lines of feminine-ended iambic pentameter or trimeter, with all stanzas in any one canzone identical. Each stanza is divided into a *fronte* (head), made of two matching *piedi* (feet) and a *sirma* (tail), sometimes divided into two *volte*. Canzone generally contain between three and seven stanzas. The opening stanza introduces a lyrical theme, the following stanzas elaborate on it, and the final stanza (sometimes just a *sirma*) concludes. The last line of a stanza often rhymes with the first line of the next.

In his translation of *Of The Gentle Heart* by Guido Guinicelli [1225–76], Dante Gabriel Rossetti [1828–82] shortens the 7- and 11-syllable Italian lines to 6 and 10 syllables to better suit English:

CANZONE - iambic pentameter/trimeter (○●) di dúm × 5/3

2. The fíre| of Lóve| comes tó| the gén|tle héart	(10)	[a]	PIEDE
Like ás| its vír|tue tó| a pré|cious stóne;	(10)	[b]	
To whích| no stár| its ín|fluence cán| impárt	(10)	[a]	PIEDE
Till ít| is máde| a púre| thing bý| the sún	(10)	[b]	
For whén| the sún| hath smít	(6)	[c]	VOLTE
From óut| its éss|ence thát| which thére| was víle,	(10)	[d]	
The stár| endów|eth ít.	(6)	[c]	
And só| the héart| creá|ted bý| God's bréath	(10)	[e]	VOLTE
Pure, trúe,| and cléan| from gúile,	(6)	[d]	
A wó|man, líke| a stár,| enám|ouréth.	(10)	[e]	

FRONTE ⊂ SIRMA

The full poem has six stanzas, each the same length and structure. Many other canzones open with a pair of quatrains, much like sonnets.

THE SAPPHIC ODE
love and devotion

The Greek poetess Sappho [c. 620–570 BC] wrote and sang oracular lyric poetry, often in three-line stanzas of mixed meter (trochee–trochee/spondee–dactyl–trochee–spondee, with an extra dactyl–spondee added to the third line). The Roman poet Horace [65–8 BC] adapted the form into Latin as three 11-syllable lines followed by a single 5-syllable line (an *adonic*). Here is a 1925 translation of Sappho's *Hymn to Aphrodite* by Edwin Marion Cox, which uses amphibrachs instead of dactyls:

Shímmer|ing-thróned| immórtal| Áphro|díté,	●○ ○● ○●○ ●○ ●●
Dáughter| of Zéus,| Enchántress,| Í imp|lóre thée,	●○ ○● ○●○ ●○ ●●
Spáre me,| Ó quéen,| this ágo|ný and| ánguish,	●○ ●● ○●○ ●○ ●●
Crúsh not my| spírit.	●○○ ●●

In English, Swinburne famously experimented with the stanza in his *Sapphics* (note the *anceps*, ☉, a foot which can be either a trochee or a spondee):

THE SAPPHIC STANZA - mixed meter

13. Sáw the\| Lésbians\| kissing a\|cróss their\| smítten
Lútes with\| líps móre\| swéet than the\| sóund of\| lúte-strings,
Móuth to\| móuth and\| hánd upon \|hánd, her\| chósen,
  Fáirer than\| áll mén;

14. Ónly| sáw the| béautiful| líps and| fíngers,	●○ ●☉ ●○○ ●○ ●☉
Fúll of| sóngs and| kísses and| líttle| whíspers,	●○ ●☉ ●○○ ●○ ●☉
Fúll of| músic;| ónly be|héld a|móng thém	●○ ●☉ ●○○ ●○ ●☉
Sóar, as a| bírd sóars	●○○ ●●

When reading a Sapphic, note how the emphasis falls more heavily in the later feet of each line.

ODES AND ELEGIES

passion, loss, lament

The modern *ode* developed from two ancient forms. The heroic *Pindaric ode*, from Pindar [522–443 BC], consists of an open-ended stanza (a *strophe*), its reverse-danced *antistrophe,* and finally a closed *epode*. Wordsworth's 1804 poem *Intimations of Immortality* encapsulates the idea within a stanza:

ENGLISH PINDARIC ODE - iambic pent./tetr./di./tri./hex.

There wás| a tíme| when méa|dow, gróve,| and stréam,	(10)	[a]	STROPHE
The eárth,| and év|ery cóm|mon síght	(8)	[b]	
To mé| did séem	(4)	[a]	ANTISTROPHE
Apparelled in celestial light,	(8)	[b]	
The glory and the freshness of a dream.	(10)	[a]	
It is not now as it hath been of yore;--	(10)	[c]	
Turn wheresoe'er I may,	(6)	[d]	EPODE
By night or day,	(4)	[d]	
The things which I have seen I now can see no more.	(12)	[c]	

The more intimate *Horatian ode* derives from Sappho via Horace and is a form of long/short line quatrain. Andrew Marvel [1621–78] shortened the first two lines to tetrameter for his *Ode upon Cromwell's Return from Ireland*:

ENGLISH HORATIAN ODE - iambic tetrameter/trimeter

He nó|thing cóm|mon díd| or méan	(8)	[a]
Upón| that mé|morá|ble scéne,	(8)	[a]
But wíth| his kée|ner éye	(6)	[b]
The áx|e's édge| did trý;	(6)	[b]

Classical *elegies* were written in *elegiac couplets*, alternate lines of dactylic hexameter (sometimes divided into halves or thirds) and pentameter.

CELTIC VERSE
the blacksmith's anvil

Irish verse is the oldest form of vernacular poetry in Europe, with the earliest written examples dating from the 6th and 7th centuries. Learned *Filidh*, seers, composed oral verse in Gaelic alongside ecclesiastical poets writing in Latin, sharing meters and forms. As with Anglo-Saxon verse (*opposite*), every line contains alliteration, with the alliterative syllables falling on stresses. Here is the 9th century poem *The Blackbird calling from the Willow*:

EARLY IRISH POEM - catalectic trochaic tetrameter (●○) dúm di × 4

ínt en| gáires| ásin| t-sáil	The bird doth from the willow speak
álainn| guílbnen| ás glan| gáir:	lovely clear-toned little beak:
rínn binn| búide fir| dúib| drúin:	yellow bill of sleek black boy:
cás cor| cúirther,| gúth ind| lúin.	bright the song, the blackbird's voice.

From the 6th to the 12th centuries, compositions often alternated sections of verse with prose (*prosimetrum*) as in *Buile Shuibne*, 'Sweeney's Frenzy', the story of a king who, cursed to madness by a saint, turns into a bird.

In the classical Bardic period [1200–1600] the traditional poetic forms were standardized, in particular the *Dan Direach*, which are composed in quatrains built from 'leading' and longer 'closing' trochaic couplets.

Later Irish poets captured some of these forms in English. Here are *hemistichs* from John Philpot Curran's [1750–1817] *The Deserter's Meditation*:

IRISH OCHTFOCLACH STANZA - catalectic dactylic dimeter (●○○) dúm diddy × 2

Bút as in| wáiling	then for that reason,
thére's nought a|váiling	and for a season
ánd death un|fáiling	let us be merry
wíll strike the| blów,	before we go.

ANGLO-SAXON VERSE
the push and pull of the oar

Anglo-Saxon verse was part of a rich, pre-Christian literary tradition of epic story, metaphysical fantasy, elegy, and magic. It is accentual with four primary stresses per line, often end-stopped, with each line divided in half with the weight of meaning in the first half. Evidence of the lolloping form survives in *Sir Gawain and the Green Knight* (late 14th C.) and *Beowulf* (8th–11th C.). Here is Beowulf's funeral (trans. Murphy & Sullivan):

ANGLO SAXON STYLE - accentual amphibrachal tetrameter

The fírewind fáltered ¶ and flámes dwíndled,	○●○ ○●○ ○●○ ○●○
hót at their héart ¶ the bróken bónehouse.	●○ ○●○ ○●○ ○●○
Her háir wáving, ¶ a Géatish wóman	○●○ ○●○ ○●○ ○●○
sáng for the Stálwart ¶ a sórrowful dírge	●○ ○●○ ○●○ ○●

Both consonants and vowels are alliterated on at least two (though typically three) of the four stressed syllables (e.g. 'fire', 'faltered', 'flames').

A figurative device, or *trope* (*see page 252*), widely used in Anglo-Saxon, Old-German and Norse verse is *kenning* (from *kenna*, 'know, feel, show'). A kenning expresses one thing in terms of another: the sea becomes the *whale-road*; the ship a *sea-steed*; the body the *bonehouse*; in the Norse *Edda*, fire is the *sun of the houses*, and arms are *mountains of hawks*. Kennings can compound, so you can have a kenning of a kenning of a kenning:

COMPOUND KENNING - from *The Names of the Hare*, c. 1200, trans. S Heaney

The stárer,| the wóod-cat,	○●○ ○●○
the púrblind,| the fúrze cat,	○●○ ○●○
the skúlker,| the bléary-eyed,	○●○ ○●○
the wáll-eyed,| the glánce aside …	○●○ ○●○

GHAZAL
song to the beloved

The *ghazal* is a poetic form originating in North Africa and the Middle-East around the 6th century. In the 12th century it spread into South Asia and India via Islam. Its theme is unrequited love, either because the love is forbidden or, especially within Sufism, the unobtainable beloved is God or a spiritual master. Ghazals frequently become intense, with the beloved referred to as a killer or assassin, and can include hyperbole and violence.

The form consists of five or more rhyming couplets and a refrain, with the last phrase of each line rhyming *aa ba ca da* etc. Notoriously hard to translate, the form is nevertheless evident in this version by Walter Leaf [1852–1927] of a ghazal by the Persian poet Hafiz of Shiraz [1316–90]:

GHAZAL - rhyming couplets in dactylic octameter, divided into hemistichs

Minstrel, awake the sound of glee; joyous and eager, fresh and free;
Fill me the bumper bounteously; joyous and eager, fresh and free.
  O for a bower and one beside; delicate dainty, there to hide;
Kisses at will to seize and be; joyous and eager, fresh and free.
  Sweet is my love, a thief of hearts; bravery, beauty, saucy arts,
Odours and unguents, all for me; joyous and eager, fresh and free.
  How shall the fruit of life be thine; if thou refuse the fruitful vine?
Drink of the wine and pledge with me; joyous and eager, fresh and free.
  Call me my Saki silver-limbed; bring me my goblet silver-rimmed;
Fain would I fill and drink to thee; joyous and eager, fresh and free.
  Wind of the West, if e'er thou roam; pass on the way my fairy's home;
Whisper of Hafiz amorously; joyous and eager, fresh and free.

The final verse of a ghazal often contains the poet's name (*as above*) or a hidden signature, a convention known as the *Maqta*.

TANKA & HAIKU
cutting through the moment

The classical *tanka* form, with its emphasis on nature, transience, and beauty, dominated Japanese poetry, or *waka*, in the 9th and 10th centuries. It has five lines with a total of 31 *on* (syllables) in the pattern: 5-7-5-7-7. From the 10th to 17th centuries the form became collaborative, as *renga*. A renga stanza splits the tanka into three opening lines, a *hokku*, plus two contrasting lines written by someone else, as shown in the verse below (*right*), taken from a longer *Haikai no renga* by master Sogi and his disciples.

TANKA - Ono no Komachi [825-900]

Though I go to you [5]
ceaselessly along dream paths, [7]
the sum of those trysts [5]
is less than a single glimpse [7]
granted in the waking world. [7]

RENGA - Inō Sogi [1421-1502]

Some snow still remains
as haze moves low on the slopes
  toward evening.   - Sogi
Flowing water, far away
and a plum-scented village.   - Shohaku

By the 13th century, rules stated that a hokku must include a *kigo* (season word), appropriate to the season in which the renga was written, e.g. 'frog' for spring or 'rain' for summer, and also a *kireji* (cutting word) which, if placed at the end of a verse provides closure or return, but when used in the middle of a verse briefly cuts the stream of thought. By the time of Matsuo Bashō [1644–1694], the hokku had begun to appear as an independent poem, the 5-7-5-*on haiku*, which keeps a sense of 'opening without a closure'.

HAIKU - Matsuo Bashō

By the ancient pond [5]
A frog jumping into it [7]
The sound of water [5]

HAIKU - Yosa Buson [1716-84]

An evening cloudburst —
sparrows cling desperately
to trembling bushes

POETIC DEVICES
rhetoric in verse

Rhetorical devices (or *figures*) are ways of patterning words, phrases, sentences and lines of verse to create deeper symmetry, meaning, and beauty. Studied by orators as persuasive aids, they are also widely used by poets to enhance the vitality of their verses.

Repetition is the most common device, whether as *refrain*, *rhyme*, or *rhythm*, or as repeated consonants, in *alliteration* and *consonance* (e.g. five/feet and blank/think), or as *assonance* in vowels (e.g. black/hat) (*see too pages 26–7*).

ALLITERATION ON 'B▸TTER'

Betty Botter bought some butter, but she said, the butter's bitter
If I put it in my batter it will make my batter bitter …

Other common repetitions include *anaphora* (where several lines begin the same way), and *polyptoton* (when a word is used in more than one way, e.g. *'Please, please me'*). In *chiasmus*, from the Greek letter X (*chi*), sounds, words, phrases and grammar are repeated in reverse order:

CHIASMUS

The wave of the particle   *I mean what I say*   *Swift as an arrow flying*

is the particle of the wave   *and I say what I mean*   *fleeing like a hare afraid*

The first two examples reverse nouns and verbs, respectively, and exhibit *antimetabole*, total symmetry, while the third inverts adjective-simile-participle into participle-simile-adjective. Entire verses of the King James Bible, *Sir Gawain and the Green Knight* and Homer's *Odyssey* and *Iliad* are structured in this way, giving them a feeling of necessary balance.

Another family of figurative devices uses repetition to compare one thing to another, using *colour*, *imagery*, and *sensory clues* to invoke memories, and *simile* ('as' or 'like') and *metaphor* to draw parallels, e.g.:

METAPHOR - from *As You Like It* by William Shakespeare, [pub. 1623]

All the world's a stage,
And all the men and women merely players;

Words sometimes sound like the things they describe, a device known as *onomatopoeia*. Similarly, *portmanteau* mixes two words into one new one:

ONOMATOPOEIA & PORTMANTEAU - from *Jabberwocky* by Lewis Carroll [1872]

Twas brillig, and the slithy toves / did gyre and gimble in the wabe
All mimsy were the borogoves, / and the mome raths outgrabe.

Poets often extend comparisons via the human *personification* of animals, objects or ideas, e.g. 'the wind whispered'. Sometimes these personifications may even be addressed directly, as in *apostrophe* (e.g. 'O Moon!'):

APOSTROPHE - from *Holy Sonnet 10* by John Donne [1572–1631]

Death, be not proud, though some have called thee
Mighty and dreadful, for thou are not so;

Occasionally, the best way to draw a comparison is by *contrast*, which in its most binary form takes the form "not X". In *antithesis* (or juxtaposition) opposing situations are overlapped for effect, e.g.:

ANTITHESIS - *Eternity* by William Blake [1757–1827]

He who binds to himself a joy / Does the wingèd life destroy
He who kisses the joy as it flies / Lives in eternity's sun rise.

Poetic devices are the secret tools which poets use to enchant their audiences, but every poem still needs *atmosphere* (mood) and symbolic *narrative*, and at the core of every poem is the poet, with their unique creative and artistic *voice*. I hope these pages help you find yours!

GLOSSARY

ACATALECTIC: Where a line contains the correct number of syllables for its meter (c.f. catalectic and acephalous).

ACCENTUAL VERSE: Rhythmic construction where only the stresses in each line are counted: e.g. Anglo-Saxon and much contemporary verse.

ACCENTUAL-SYLLABIC VERSE: Rhythmic construction where both the number of syllables and stresses are counted in each line of verse.

ACEPHALOUS (Lit. headless): Lacking a syllable or syllables in the first foot of a line (= headless line), (c.f. catalectic and acatalectic).

ACROSTIC: A form where the first letter of each line of a poem spells a word. Also mesostic, middle of the line, and telestich, end of the line.

ALLITERATION: A form of consonance; the repetition of stressed consonant sounds at the beginning of words (e.g. 'As kingfishers catch fire, dragonflies draw flame' - G.M.Hopkins).

AMPHIMACER (Lit. long at both ends): (=cretic). A metrical foot of one unstressed syllable between two stressed ones (e.g. dum di dum).

AMPHIBRACH (Lit. short on both sides): A metrical foot of one stressed syllable between two unstressed syllables (e.g. di dum di).

ANCEPS: A variable metrical unit, normally either a trochee or a spondee.

ANAPEST (Lit. struck back): A metrical foot of two unstressed syllables followed by one stressed syllable (e.g. di di dum).

ANGLO-SAXON VERSE: Accentual verse with 4 stresses per line. Lines are hemistich - in two halves, separated by caesura. No rhyme, alliteration on 2-3 primary stresses.

APOSTROPHE (app-os-tro-FEE): An exclamatory passage in addressed to an imaginary person/abstract entity. Often begins with 'O' (e.g. 'O death, where is thy sting?').

ASSONANCE: Repeating vowel sounds in successive words (e.g. do you like blue?).

BALLAD: A narrative poem in short, usually four line, stanzas; was often song. In pop music the term now refers to an emotive or dramatic love song.

BALLADE: French verse form of three 8-line stanzas and a 4-line envoi, rhyming ababbcbC, bcbC.

BEDLAMITE VERSE: Poems in the voice of 'Poor Tom' or his sweetheart 'Merry Mad Maud'.

BLANK VERSE: Open form of non-stanzaic verse, unrhymed and usually in iambic pentameter. Appears frequently in plays of Shakespeare and poems of Milton.

CAESURA: A significant pause (often for breath) in a line of verse, usually marked with a comma, colon or semi-colon.

CATALECTIC: Lacking one or more syllables in the first, or more often last, foot of a line (c.f. acephalous and acatalectic).

CHAIN RHYME: Interlinking stanzas by carrying rhymes over from one stanza to the next (e.g. aba bcb cdc ded...).

CHORIAMB: A metrical foot of two stressed syllables sandwiched by two unstressed syllables.

CLOSED FORM: Any poetic form where meter, stanza, rhyme, and other features are all fixed (= fixed form).

CONTRACTION: Reducing the number of syllables in a word (= elision), (q.v. syncope and synaeresis).

CONSONANCE: The repetition of consonant sounds in successive words (e.g. tomorrow matters for Timmy, the end well found), (c.f alliteration).

COUPLET: A 2-line rhyming stanza in any meter.

DACTYL (DACK-till, Gr. finger): A metrical foot of one stressed syllable followed by two unstressed syllables; dum di di.

DIPODIC VERSE: Strongly metrical verse with only two feet per line. Rap lyrics are often dipodic.

DISTICH: A unit of two verse lines, usually a couplet.

ELISION: The omission of one or more sounds (vowel, consonant, or syllable) from words or phrases, often used to aid adherence to a metrical scheme or rhythm (e.g. oft, o'er), (q.v. syncope and synaeresis).

ELLIPSIS: Dropping words without impeding the reader's ability to understand meaning (e.g. 'I will away').

ENDSTOPPING: When a line of verse ends without running on (grammatically) to the next.

ENJAMBMENT: When a line runs or 'strides' into the next (e.g. I sing it in / My heart this / Joyful song).

EPENTHESIS: The addition of a sound to a word.

EPIC VERSE: Long and often dramatic narrative poetry with grand, noble, mythological, or nationally important themes (c.f. lyric poetry).

FEMININE RHYME: *Rhymes the second from last syllables of successive words.*

FEMININE ENDING: *A line of verse which ends on an unstressed syllable.*

FREE VERSE: *Poetry with no conventional meter or form.*

FOOT: *A metrical unit, comprised of stressed and unstressed syllables, in varying combinations, used to measure and represent poetic meter. The system is inherited from ancient Greek literature and the different metrical feet retain their Greek names (e.g iamb, dactyl, anapest, etc.).*

GNOMIC POETRY: *Verse containing short statements (gnomes) pertaining to general truth or morality (e.g. 'Thus did Ecgtheow's son, so famous for battles and valient deeds, act as a brave man ought' - Beowulf).*

HAIKU: *Japanese poetic form. Three lines of 5-7-5 'on' (approximate to syllables). Syllabic meter. No rhyme. Used for meditative/lyrical/transcendental themes.*

HEADLESS: *See ACEPHALOUS.*

HETEROMETRIC STANZA: *A stanza with lines containing different numbers of syllables (c.f. isometric stanza).*

HEMISTICH: *A half-line of verse followed and preceded by a caesura.*

HEPTAMETER: *A metrical line of seven feet.*

HEXAMETER: *A metrical line of six feet.*

HOLORHYME: *A line/stanza that rhymes in its entirety (e.g. Ms Stephen, without a first-rate stakeholder sum or deal / Must, even, with outer fur straight, stay colder, some ordeal).*

HYPERCATALECTIC: *A metrical line of verse which contains an additional syllable or syllables (c.f. acephalous and acatalectic).*

IAMB: *A metrical foot containing one unstressed syllable followed by one stressed syllable (e.g. beSIDE).*

ISOMETRIC STANZA: *A stanza with lines containing equal numbers of syllables.*

LAISSE: *A stanza of varying length; each line typically decasyllabic or alexandrine; found in medieval French epic poetry. Line-endings are assonant rather than rhyming (e.g. 'The Song of Roland').*

LIMERICK: *A 5-line rhyming poem, usually with an anapestic or amphibrachic meter.*

LINEATION: *The manner in which line breaks are inserted in a poem for expressive/rhythmical purposes.*

LINKED VERSE: *Poems written collectively by more than one person (often in large groups, e.g. renga).*

LYRIC POETRY (ENGLISH): *Poetry expressing personal thoughts or feelings, typically spoken in first person (c.f. epic verse).*

LYRIC POETRY (GREEK): *Ancient Greek verse sung to music played on the lyre ('lyrikos' = adj. form of 'lyra').*

MAD SONG: *A verse form of 5-line stanzas. Variable accentual meter. Rhymes abccb etc. Used for nonsense, oddities and madness.*

MASCULINE RHYME: *Rhymes the last syllable of each word.*

MASCULINE ENDING: *A line of verse which ends on a stressed syllable.*

METER: *The measurement of regular rhythm in verse.*

MIMESIS: *'To imitate'. In ancient Greek poetics, the process by which the arts come to truth through imitation and stylization of humanity and nature.*

OCTAMETER: *A metrical line of eight feet.*

OCTAVE: *Any eight-line stanza, although most often two quatrains, the first eight lines of a sonnet.*

ODE: *An elaborately structured poem praising or glorifying an event or individual.*

ON: *Japanese phonetic units similar to English syllables but different in that they can contain two distinct sounds.*

OPEN FORM: *Metrical poetry with no fixed rhyme or stanza scheme (c.f. closed form, blank verse, free verse).*

OTTAVA RIMA: *A rhyming stanza form, originally from Italy, of 8 lines, usually in iambic pentameter.*

PALINDROME: *A device used since antiquity where a word, phrase, number or sequence reads the same backwards as forwards. Earliest from 79 AD Herculaneum (e.g. 'noon', 'race car', 'able was I ere I saw Elba', 'madam, I'm Adam').*

PANTOUM: *Malayan closed verse form adapted to English.*

PAEAN (PEE-uhn): *A song/chant of praise, triumph, or imploration.*

PAEON (PEE-uhn): *A type of quaternary foot.*

PENTAMETER: *A metrical line of five feet.*

PETRARCHAN SONNET: *Sonnet form named for Francesco Petrarca [1304-74]. Two quatrains (an octave) followed by a sestet.*

PROSODY: *The study of poetic meter and the art of versification.*

PYRRHIC (Pee-rik): *A metrical foot of two unstressed syllables.*

QUALITATIVE VERSE: *Poetry which counts stressed syllables at regular intervals as either the only (accentual) or combined (accentual-syllabic) component of its meter.*

QUANTITATIVE VERSE: *The type of metrical poetry*

written in Ancient Greek (and other syllable-timed languages) which counts syllable length, not stress.

QUATRAIN: A stanza of four lines.

RENGA: Japanese collaborative poetry, opening stanza developed into Haiku form.

RHYME ROYAL: A 7-line stanza of iambic pentameter, rhyming ababbcc. Originally a medieval French form introduced into English poetry by Chaucer.

RONDEAU: A French verse form with various English adaptations. Usually consists of 12 or 15 lines in 2 or 3 rhyming stanzas with a refrain.

RUBAI / RUBA'IYAT: Verse form originally from Persia in quatrains rhyming aaba ccdc dded etc.

SAPPHIC ODE: English ode form adapted from the Sapphic stanza via Roman poet Horace who added a 5-syllable fourth line.

SAPPHIC STANZA: Hendecasyllabic (11 syllables per line) metrical / stanzaic scheme originally used by celebrated Greek lyric poetess Sappho [c.630-570 BC]; 3 lines, 5 feet per line, usually: trochee, trochee or spondee, dactyl, trochee, spondee. (= Sapphic meter).

SCANSION: The process of determining and representing (usually graphically) the metrical nature of verse.

SESTINA: A closed verse form of six 6-line stanzas with a 3-line envoi at the end. Accentual-syllabic meter of any length. Normally no rhyme.

SHAKESPEAREAN SONNET: A sonnet in iambic pentameter, three quatrains and a couplet (= English sonnet).

SONNET: A 14-line poem following various schemes and conventions; usually expressing affairs of the heart. Originally from 13th C. Italy.

SPONDEE: A metrical foot of two stressed syllables.

STANZA: The dividing unit of a poem comprised of a fixed number of lines, often arranged in a metrical pattern.

STICH (STIK): A line of poetry.

STICHIC (STIK-ik): Of, or in, lines only, as opposed to stanzas. Also, 'lines' as opposed to sentences - the difference between poetry and prose. (c.f. strophic)

STROPHE: Lit a "turn, bend, twist". Originally the first part of an ode in Greek tragedy. Now the term is usually considered equivalent to "stanza". Can also refer to a shift from one kind of metrical foot to another.

STROPHIC: Poetry composed in stanzas as distinct from epic poems or blank verse which are composed in lines.(c.f stichic), (= stanzaic).

STRESS: The emphasis of syllables in spoken language by

variation of some or all of the following: pitch, loudness, length and timbre.

SUBSTITUTION: Swapping, or substituting, one kind of metrical foot for another in lines of verse.

SYLLABIC VERSE: Poetic construction where only the number of syllables are counted in each line. Line breaks are often arbitrary/imperceptible when read aloud.

SYNAERESIS (see-NEA-ry-sys): Joining two vowels to create a single syllable (e.g. 'of man's first disobedience', Di-so-be-di-ence becomes di-so-be-dyence to preserve Milton's pentameter).

SYNCOPE (SIN-kuh-pee): A form of elision; the omission from a word of either a consonant (e.g. 'ne'er') or unstressed vowel (e.g. 'hastening' to 'hast'ning').

SYZYGY (SIZ-ee-jee): Can refer to the combination of two metrical feet into one (e.g. iamb + trochee = choriamb).

TANKA: Traditional Japanese 5-line poem.

TERZA RIMA: Open form of 3-line stanzas in pentameter, rhyming aba bab cdc ded efe... ee. Used in Dante's 'Divine Comedy'. Narrative and lyrical.

TETRAMETER: A metrical line of four feet.

THORN LINE: A line without rhyme in a generally rhymed passage. There are ten 'thorn lines' among the 193 lines in Milton's irregularly rhymed 'Lycidas'.

TRIMETER: A metrical line of three feet.

TRIOLET: Closed form of 8 lines of accentual-syllabic verse with any meter. Rhymes ABaAabAB (A+B = refrains). Used for lyrical/light verse/imagistic themes.

TRIPLET/TERCET: 3-line stanzas of any meter, rhyming aaa/aba. Semantically linked , often a complete statement

TROCHEE (TRO-key): A metrical unit (or "foot") containing one stressed syllable followed by one unstressed syllable (e.g. STATEment, RIVer, WONder).

TROPE: A device (or 'figure') which uses words in a non-literal sense. Tropes commonly used in poetry include metaphor, metonymy and simile.

VERSE: Poetry as distinct from prose. The word 'verse' is used interchangeably with 'poetry'. Also a traditional word for stanza.

VERSIFICATION: The art or technique of writing verse.

VILLANELLE: A 19 line poem (6 stanzas of 3 lines each) with rhyming refrains and a concluding quatrain, all in iambic pentameter. Also a French dance with sung lyrics.

VIRELAI: A French verse form often used in song and dance.

WRENCHED ACCENT: The forcing of an accent onto a non-accented syllable (e.g. 'in my imagination' becomes 'in my imagina-shee-aan').